CONTENTS

Read each walk and study each map before you star
8. Walks are found on OS Explorer 145 or 146. Av

INTRODUCTION & USEFUL INFO

This is a country of outstanding beauty, blessed with thousands of miles of footpaths. There is always more to discover, we never know what we'll see next, and nothing ever looks the same.

Far from being a waste of time, walking is therapeutic; an antidote to the wear and tear of modern living. Chemicals called endorphins which make us feel good are manufactured by the brain during exercise, and the effect can last for hours after we've stopped.

As well as a source of pleasure and health, walking can be quality time with family or friends, and on your own, valuable thinking, planning and ideas time.

WEATHER Don't be put off too easily. It's seldom wet all day every day and forecasts are often wrong. We need to get out, especially in winter, and the country side can look great any time of year. ITV teletext 152, 153 weather guide is often more accurate than BBC2 ceefax 401 and 403.

WET WEATHER WALKING Few people enjoy slipping and sliding for miles in mud. Some of these walks are good in wet weather. Norbury Park and Albury Park areas have some good wet weather walking.

MAPS Reading a map is not difficult. It takes a little time and practise to master, but will give great pleasure. Then the world's your oyster. Maps are not 100% accurate, and not every path that is on the ground is on the map, and vice versa.

LAND MARKS CHANGE Some stiles are being replaced by kissing gates. Trees come down. Buildings go up or are removed. New fences are put in. Even in a different season, or in the opposite direction, the same walk may look like another planet. Vandals may remove markers and maps. **Be observant**. Look ahead for wooden footpath posts, marker arrows and stiles or gates. Look for footpaths that have been worn by feet across grass or fields.

DIVERSIONS Footpaths are sometimes diverted. Inform the council's Rights of Way Officer or your local Ramblers group if you think a legal path has been blocked.

PACE Natural walking pace is different for everyone. It can be tiring to walk too slow or too fast. Anyone can increase their pace and fitness with regular practise. **Hills** are always worth the effort. Take your time.

FARM ANIMALS Keep clear of livestock. Never feed or touch them. If they're a bit lively, stand still and talk to them in a low pitched, loud calm voice.

Cows with calves can be aggressive if they think their young are at risk. Don't walk between mother and baby. Most cattle don't like dogs. You may occasionally be at risk if you have a dog with you, even on a lead.

Cattle and cows are naturally nosy, associating people with food. Don't be alarmed if they follow you. Do not run from a herd of cattle. If you run they may also, and could accidentally run you down.

Bulls—Farmers are liable if someone is hurt by a dangerous bull in a field with a public footpath. So it's unlikely (but not impossible) they'll put one there. Sometimes there will be a warning 'BULL'. Usually he's in with cows and has eyes only for them. Just keep an eye on him.

FOOTWEAR Every foot is different. If you walk often, you need a strong comfortable shoe or boot, not too heavy, with a good tread, preferably water proof, and quality socks.

Walking In Wellies. If you love to walk all seasons but find mud and puddles off-putting I urge you to try wellies. 'Oh No' you say 'I could never walk in wellies.' I said the same but find I can walk comfortably for 6-8 miles, and not fuss every step. It's fun paddling and easy to clean afterwards.

Tips—Buy a size larger (warm feet swell) with good tread. Insert a quality inner-sole.

Wear two pairs of socks (one thin), tuck your trousers into them - the 2nd long and thicker - turn them over the tops of your wellies.

ROADS AND OTHER TRAFFIC

Cars. Are you a rambling road hog? Many walkers in larger groups are oblivious of cars when walking along minor roads. This is a) dangerous and b) very irritating to drivers.
Bicycles mostly don't seem to carry bells any more. Keep one ear open.
Horses are unpredictable. If you meet horses and riders, give them a wide berth. It's probably best to stop while they pass. If in doubt ask the rider.
Epsom Downs—On Epsom Downs stay well away from horses on the race course or training gallops (usually am's only). They're highly strung, accidents easily happen, and you could be liable.

GENERAL TIPS

- Walking the walk in opposite direction Make notes the first time you do the walk by looking behind you every 100 yds or so.
- Walking stick—useful for anyone, any age in steep or slippery conditions.
- Secateurs often handy
- Wet wood is nearly always slippery.

WHAT YOU MIGHT NEED Bum bags/day pack, light plastic to sit on, map case and map. Water. Fruit. Tissues. Plasters Spare plastic bag/s for dirty boots or litter, or sitting on.

CLOTHING Wear layers—so you can take off or put on as you need. Keep spare water proof, hat, gloves, scarf, socks, shoes in car.

HEALTH Any walking for a sustained period is healthy (except along a busy road!). Experts say we actually burn more fat walking at a slower pace.

WEIGHT If you'd like to lose weight, once a week won't do it—you need to exercise 30 minutes every day and adjust diet. If you'd like to increase your fitness, 15 mins a day brisk walking will help.

CAR PARKS Thieves know car parks. **Never leave any valuables in your car**. Leave cabin empty and handbags at home.

INITIALS

NSEW	North south east west
PO	Post office
NDW	North Downs Way
OS	Ordnance Survey
PF FP	Public Footpath footpath
CP	Car park
LHS	Left hand side RHS right hand side
NT	National Trust
SCC	Surrey County Council
P	Page
SSA	Philips Surrey Street Atlas
MV	Mole Valley
OS SSA	Philips Ordnance Survey SSA

GUIDED WALKS Surrey's Environment News (a free SCC paper available from libraries April and September) has a programme of informative guided walks. There are Ramblers groups in every county. U3A and GO 50 have regular walks programmes. Info on walks and local history at libraries.

USEFUL CONTACTS

BT Conservation Volunteers	020 8541 7157
Mole Valley Council	01306 885001
Mole Valley Ramblers	01372 361011
Rights of Way	020 8541 9331
Surrey County Council	020 8541 9432
Surrey Wildlife Trust	01483 488055

PUBLIC TRANSPORT For up to date information on bus/train services contact your local library, or phone Traveline 08706 082608

COUNTRYSIDE GUIDELINES

- Leave gates as you find them
- Keep dogs under control, and always on a lead near farm animals
- Keep to paths, especially on farm land—do not short cut over fields
- Take your rubbish home

1. LEATHERHEAD TO BOCKETTS FARM

Easy, 3 miles. Impassable when river's high
Combine with Walk 2 for 5 mile walk

Maps SSA P69 F4 OS SSA p 95 B5
Start Leatherhead Library
Best when dry, wellies / boots if wet

Walk out from the library to main road, turn right immediately and head downhill on Vicarage Lane, a rough lane that runs between the Mansion and Hutchinson's Fire Shop. When you reach an arch in the wall right, go through it and follow path and steps down to river.

With river left, walk along footpath to bridge. Cross bridge, and immediately after crossing, turn left on to another footpath. Stay on this path which runs beside the river until you reach Thorncroft Drive.

Turn right and follow this lane, passing Thorncroft Manor right. After passing several cottages left and right, you'll reach the rifle range gates (at end of high brick wall) left. Turn left along footpath which again takes you close to the river. Stay on this path, passing under Young Street.

Keep to the river edge path until you reach a kissing gate. Do not go through. Instead, turn right and with your back to the river, walk slowly uphill past picnic tables, then car park right. Pass under a railway bridge, walk up several steps to another kissing gate, then continue half way up the hill.

When you reach a line of trees right, turn right with the path and walk along this tunnel of trees until the path again turns left and uphill. You will see a wooden gate and stile. Climb over the stile and follow the farm track to Bocketts Farm. (Opportunity for Lunch or snack—very family friendly. Delightful in spring with all the baby animals.)

Continue on same track, (past the farm car park left), which curves right and brings you to Young Street. Cross over to bridleway which continues through a wooded area for about ½ a mile.

After this you will come to an open field right. When the field ends, turn right downhill.

Follow the bridleway, which runs left, then right across a railway bridge. Continue on down the rocky track. Left, you'll soon see the Leisure Centre, right a vineyard. You are again in Thorncroft Drive, which leads past Thorncroft Manor.

At the river you can either retrace your steps beside the river, or cross the bridge, turn left and walk along the busy main road back to library (not so pleasant).

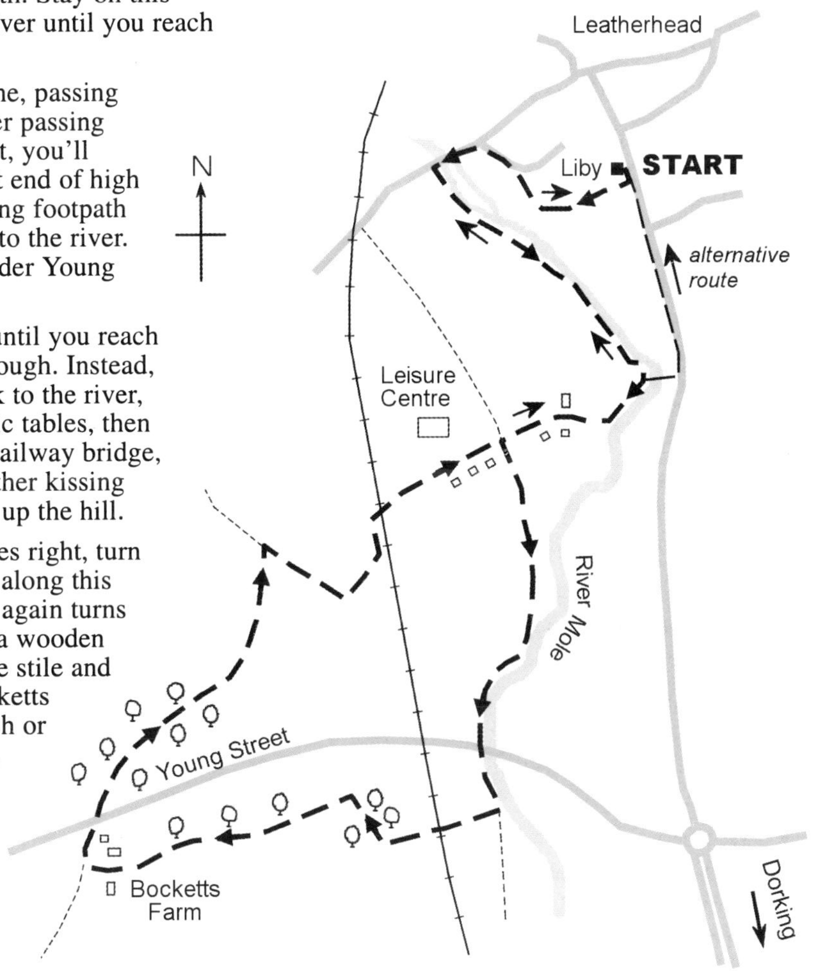

2. LEATHERHEAD TO ICEHOUSE COMBE

Undulating, 3¼ miles. Impassable when river's high

Maps SSA P70 A4 OS SSA p 95 B5

Start at Parish Church, Leatherhead
Parking in Swan Centre CP, or Church Street CP or behind the Parish Church Hall.

Combine with Walk One for 5 mile walk

Make your way to St Marys and St Nicholas' Church on the corner of Church Street and Church Road.

Walk up Church Road and immediately where boundary of church ends, turn right into Worple Lane. Walk the full length of the lane. At the Tee junction, turn right and walk down to Downs Lane.

Turn left up Downs Lane and walk past Downside Manor left and Downside Cottage right. Follow this lane, which becomes a bridleway only, up and over the hill (past Highfields Cottage) and down to the A24.

Across the road you will see the entrance to Givons Grove via Crabtree Drive. Cross carefully and walk into Crabtree Dr and take first right which is Garden Close. After a few hundred yards this turns sharply uphill. Continue up hill to T Junction, then turn left. The ascent is gentle now.

Keep an eye on the house names on your right. Between Beech Fell and Seven Cables turn right down a grassy track. Follow this path to the A24. The last house on right just before the A24 is Hunters Combe. Take right fork to roadside and cross south bound carriage way there. Mind your step down the uneven bank to cycle path.

At this point you will see an illegible sign edged with luminous tape, on the other side of the north bound carriageway. (Once across the road, take this entrance.) However, before crossing, walk right along cycle path until you can see oncoming traffic clearly. This is a blind bend with 2 lanes of cars approaching at great speed.

Once you have crossed, walk back to sign and walk down access road to river. Cross the bridge and after 20–30 paces, at junction of two tracks, turn right towards a wide gate. Go through and keep to rough farm track.

The river is now on your right and you're heading in the direction of Leatherhead. On your left are fields, sometimes with horses and donkeys. When the track swings right after Icehouse Cottage (or Lilac Cottage) on your left, follow it.

At the end of a long flat straight stretch there is a slight rise and at the top of this rise you will find yourself looking down at the river, with a green field stretching in front of you.

Follow the obvious well walked path through the green field until you reach a wooden kissing gate at the far end of the field, once again right beside the river. Keeping the river right, follow the path under an arched bridge.

Keep to this level path, with a vineyard and flat field left, until you reach a kissing gate and Thorncroft Lane. Turn right here and walk to the river.

At the river you can either turn left and walk beside the river to next bridge. Crossing this 2nd bridge will lead you straight back in to Leatherhead. Or cross Thorncroft bridge, turn left and walk along the busy main road back to library (not so pleasant).

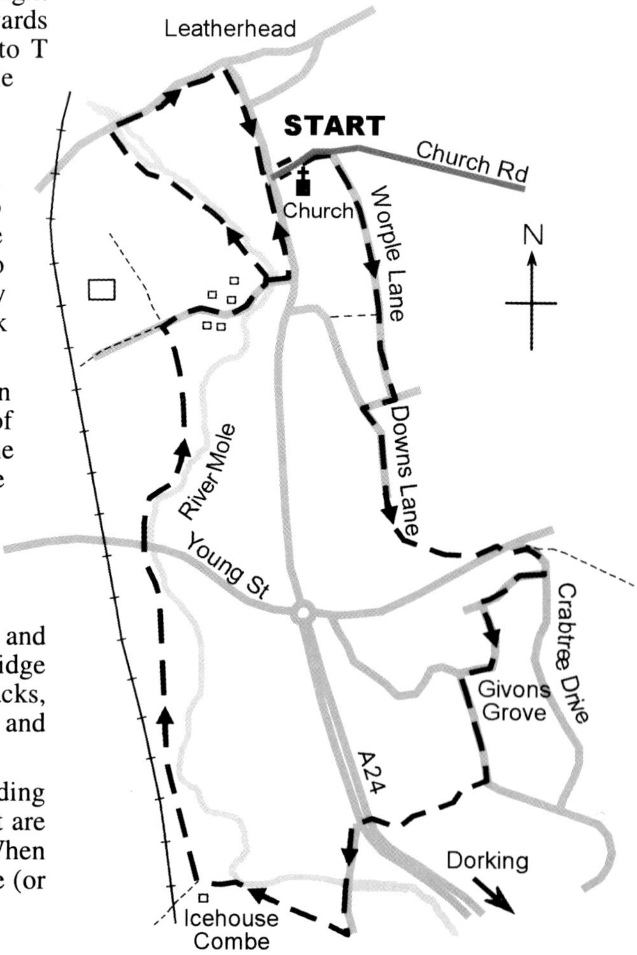

3. WINE, VENISON AND THE NORTH DOWNS WAY

Easy, undulating 3½ miles **or** 5 miles from Ryka's CP
Mostly good underfoot. Magnificent views on a clear day

Maps SSA P87 D4 OS SSA p115 C3 OS
Start Boxhill Stepping Stones CP

Travelling on the A24 in the direction of Dorking from the Burford Bridge roundabout, the car park is about 1/3 of a mile on your left immediately after a bus stop. (The car park sign is not obvious.) If you reach the Denbies roundabout you've gone too far.

Cross the A24 with care. You will see imposing gateposts and gate at the start of a lane not quite opposite the carpark's entrance. At the entrance of the lane is a wooden footpath marker saying North Downs Way. Walk up this lane, under a railway bridge and past a shaded cottage left.

At Denbies wooden gate you'll see the acorn sign which is the symbol of the NDW. Keep to this track. After 200 yds or so you will see Denbies buildings left across the vineyard. From here the path levels out.

When you reach a four way intersection, pause to enjoy the view of Box Hill, Denbies and Dorking. Remember this intersection for later. The bridleway up hill to your right will be part of your return journey.

Continue on the same track, still on the North Downs Way, and now curving slowly right. You will soon emerge from the trees to have a clear view left of Dorking and west towards Westcott.

At high metal gates (sometimes open, sometime closed), leave them as you find them. Continue up hill, a deer enclosure right, and vines on a steep slope left

You will come to a second large metal gate. About 100 yards after this you will reach a junction. Turn right up a rise, still following the acorn sign, a white cottage ahead left.

At the T junction just past this cottage turn right on to a wide concrete drive. Walk along this drive, past the 'Dairy Cottages' right. Continue on this farm track passing 'The Forts' and 'Ashcombe Cottage'.

Just past the last cottage, as the track narrows you will see a wooden footpath sign with a yellow arrow, pointing downhill. (It's all downhill from here!) This track is rough, rocky and steep, so a good idea to go slow. A stick is an asset for any age.

At Tee junction, (when your knees are creaking) turn right on to a wider track, still downhill. You will come to the familiar junction with the view of Boxhill, Denbies and Dorking. Walk straight on down into the vineyard towards the buildings. (The grass verge right of the track is more comfortable under foot.)

When the buildings are almost directly in front of you, turn left along a grassy (or muddy) path between rows of vines. This leads you out of the estate and back to the NDW. Turn right and retrace your steps to the car park.

For a 5 mile walk, start at the public CP near Burford Bridge roundabout and follow the peaceful grassy bend in the river, which will add 1/2 an hour to the walk.

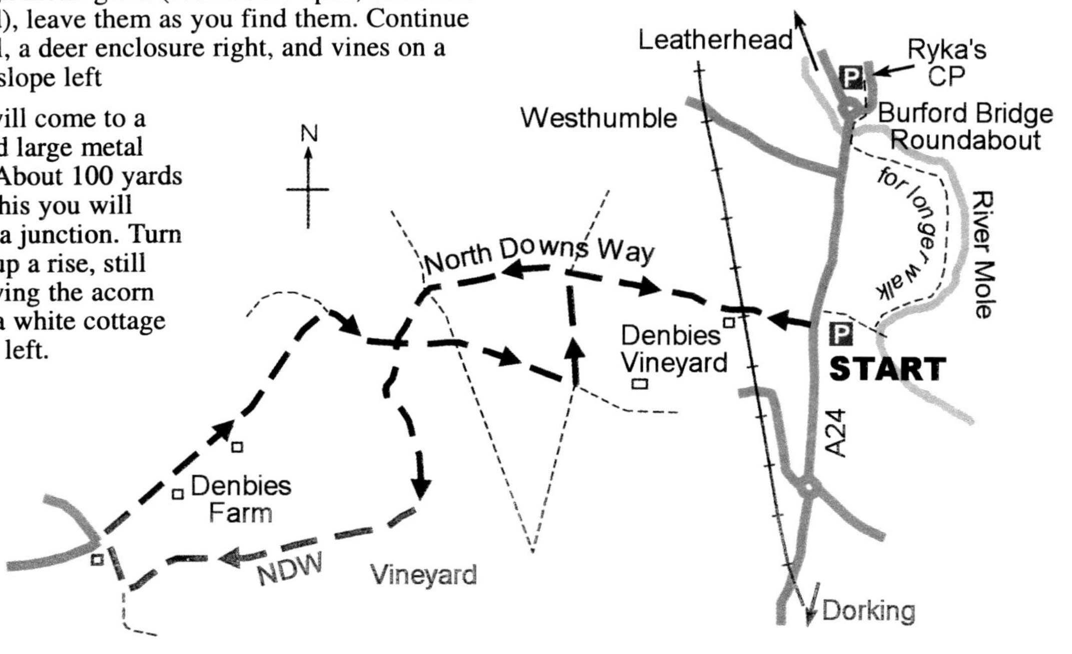

4. ON TOP OF THE WORLD — NOWER WOOD & THE GALLOPS

Undulating, 3 miles. Dry weather walk

Maps SSA P87 F1 OS SSA p96 A2
Start at Nower Wood CP

Nower Wood CP is on the B2033 (Mill Way). Coming from the roundabout at Leatherhead bypass, you'll pass Tyrrell's Wood Golf course on both left and right sides of the road. The CP is on your right at the crest of a hill, straight after Nower Wood Educational Nature Centre CP (well sign posted) on left.

As you stand with your back to the road, you will see a wooden fingerpost indicating 2 footpaths. Follow the left arrow on a level path that has a wooden picket-like fence left. (Don't turn right downhill.) Violets abound here. When the picket fence ends you'll see a path immediately left. Ignore it.

Instead, take a further 10–20 paces and duck under the wire strung between white fence posts. You are now at the start of a long grassy stretch called The Gallop. Take the next path on your left, downhill past a pile of cut tree logs. This path is steepish but does level out at times to give you some relief. Rest whenever you need to.

At the bottom of the hill turn right. In April you'll see and hear the lambs in the paddock to left. Slowly wend your way up hill. The path soon flattens out and the rest of the walk is easy. Sometimes it's rocky underfoot and there are many tree roots across the path. If they are wet avoid walking on them. Wet wood is always slippery.

You will pass between 2 halves of a large fallen tree. Just after this, if the trees are still bare you'll have a picturesque view of Warren Farm left and way below.

Continue on this path which is more or less straight ahead and slightly indistinct at one point where it twists through some trees. You will eventually emerge at a large clearing with a wooden seat under a tree right, and glorious views from Juniper Tops left, to the Ranmore church spire above the treetops right.

Turn sharp right at this wooden seat (you'll see a dark blue arrow on a finger post.) Walk about 10–20 yards from the wooden bench, and just past a metal corner post with no fence attached, turn left, following another blue arrow uphill.

10–20 yds along this path you'll reach a Tee junction with blue arrows pointing left and right. Turn right and stay on this easy and obvious path which will lead you back onto the gallop.

Turn right and walk (gallop if you like—it's very tempting) along this lofty stretch which feels like the top of the world, until you come again to the white posted fence you ducked under earlier. From here retrace your steps to the carpark, this time with the wooden picket-like fence right.

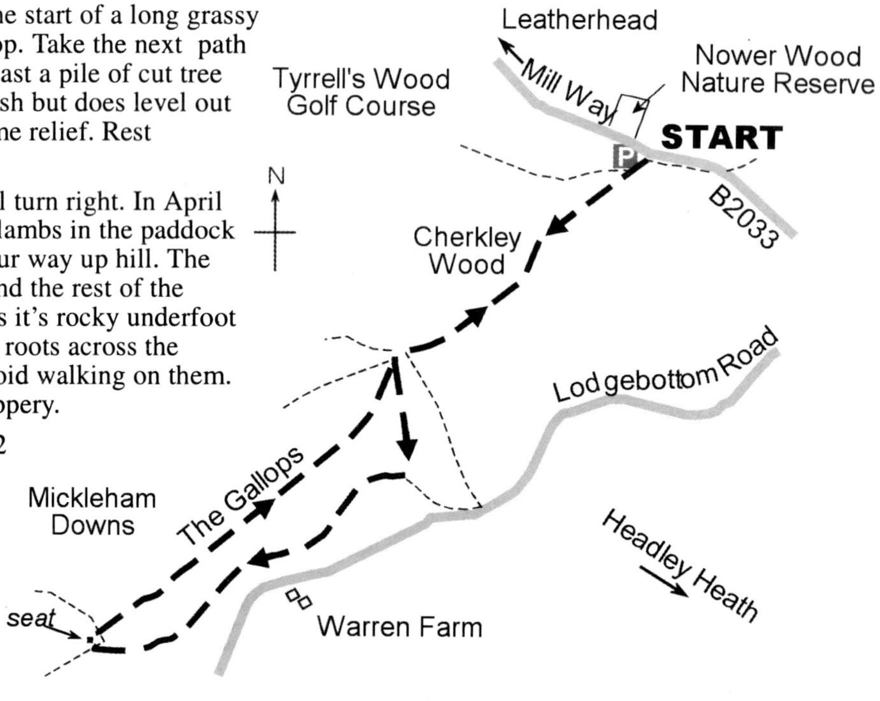

5. DOWNS WAY TO DRUIDS GROVE LOOKOUT

Easy, 2½ miles.

Maps SSA page 86. B1 OS SSA p94 D1
Start Top of Downs Way, Bookham.

Drive out of Leatherhead on the A246. At the first Bookham shops on right, prepare to turn left into Downs Way. The entrance is directly opposite the Thackray Care Centre.

Walk along the farm track which is a continuation of Down's Way. You will have open green fields left and right. In the distance left you will see the white Esso building, and on a clear day, in the far distance you will see Epsom Races Grandstand.

You will come to a footpath marker at the junction ahead. Ignore it and walk straight on, now with a hedge and woods left. Almost immediately, you'll find yourself walking easy grade downhill. You will see trees planted on the hillside ahead and slightly right.

At the Tee junction with Roaringhouse Farm left. (Mole Valley Mowers), turn left, then immediately right up a narrower diagonal track.

Just over the top of the rise, walk on along the path that is accompanied by power lines. Stay with the power lines. They will eventually lead you into a vast grassy open area. You will see a red brick cottage right. Keep on the path beside the power lines, with the cottage right, until you come to a wooden seat and a bridleway sign pointing left or right.

Turn right just before the wooden seat, along a grassy track, which soon becomes a wide (sometimes muddy) track. Follow this track as it twists through woods until you reach a narrow bitumened road. Turn left. Do not exceed the speed limit, and mind the bump!

From here it's 10 or 20 paces to a wooden sign pointing right to 'Viewpoint'. This leads you to Druids Grove lookout, with seats, picnic tables and fine views, from Mickleham left to Dorking extreme right.

Once rested, back track to the road and turn right. After 10–20 yards you will have a high wire fence on your right which is the boundary of Norbury House. At the next speed bump you will spot the house and gardens through the trees. This as you may know was once the home of Marie Stopes. Left you will see a timber mill. Turn left between the mill and the picnic table area. This track will return you to the huge open grassy area.

Here the track becomes a wide flint and gravel road. You will see the red brick cottage again, about a quarter of a mile away left. Stay on this road as it curves right and downhill, until an obvious white path dissects it diagonally.

You will see a bridleway sign. Turn left up this white path. There is a thick wooden post in the middle of the track just as you start up hill.

Do not turn left or right off this track. At the crest of the hill you will see the power lines once more. Keep walking straight on 'til you're back at Roaringhouse Farm. Walk back past the farmhouse and up the hill, to Downs Way.

On the map you can see it would be easy to add 'a corner' to the walk near the end.

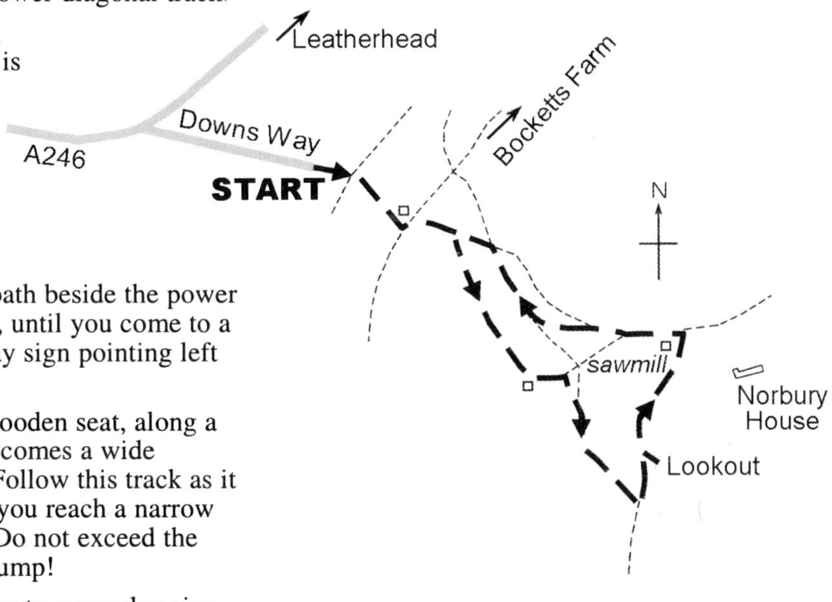

6. ASHTEAD COMMON

Easy, 3½ miles. Blossom in Spring. Usually marshy—wellies!

Maps SSA P 70 B2 OS SSA p75 E2/3
Start either at Ashtead railway station or at the bend in Broadhurst Road. If you park at the station or in Woodfield Lane, cross the railway line and keep walking down the track that lies straight ahead of you.

If you park near the bend in Broadhurst Road, there is a footpath running between No 33 and No 35. (see SSA, page 70, B1).

At the end of this footpath turn right along the edge of the common, on a path that runs parallel with the houses. When you come to a wooden barrier, (where the houses right finish), turn left, take about 10 paces then turn right on to a wide gravel path that has a deep ditch running on its left side.

At the next junction, turn left on to a rougher track, leaving the gravel path, and walk between 2 blue topped posts. You will soon see a pond left, then 2 cottages.

A short distance right you will glimpse a cycle path, running almost parallel with the path you're on but more curvaceous and well surfaced. If you prefer, walk along this track, but take care not to get run over. There doesn't seem to be such a thing as a bicycle bell any more. These paths are lined with oaks and silver birch.

Turn left at the next junction and within a few yards you will come to a sturdy white coal tax post. As you reach this post you will see an open field right, and looking across this field to the left, you will see Rushett farm, which used to be home to The Game Larder.

Continue on the same path in the same direction keeping the farm's fields right and soon reaching another coal tax post and a large sign board showing a map of the common. If you're eight foot tall, you will read this sign with ease.

Keep on along this same path until you come to a corner with a glimpse of farm buildings and horses ahead of you. (Epsom Gap Farm)

You will be quite close to the A243 and will hear the traffic. At this corner there is another large sign with another map, this time accessible for people under 8 foot.

From here it's about a mile to your transport. The rest of the walk is easy to follow. Turn left away from the farm and continue along the bridleway (a gentle incline for a short way) walking between the blue tipped posts all the way back to the railway crossing. In early spring the white blossom on this home stretch is glorious in its profusion.

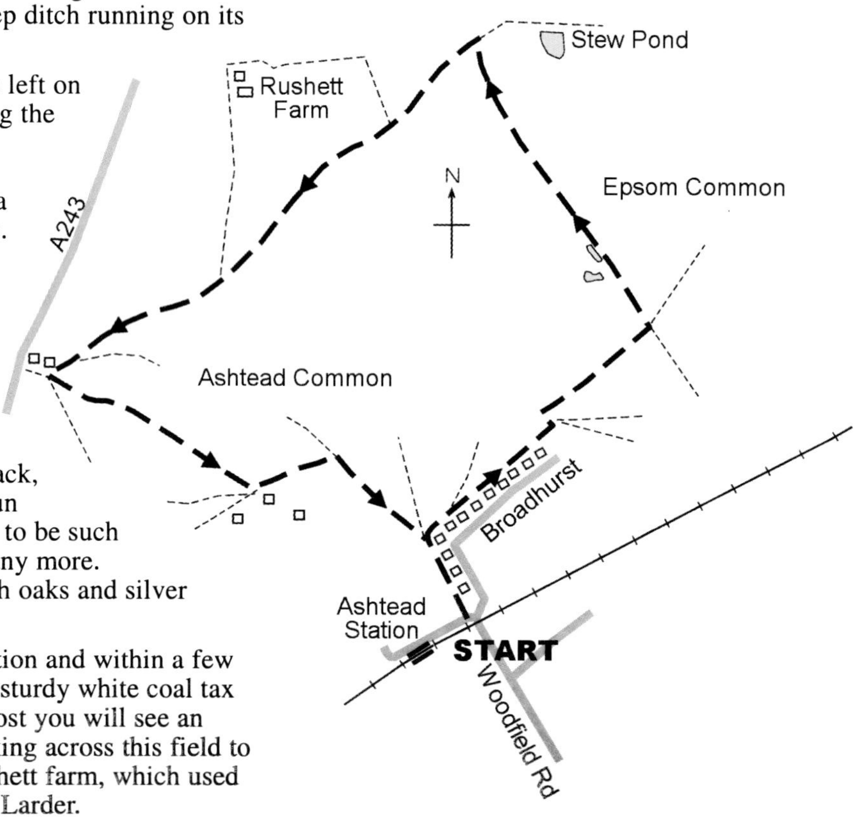

7. RANMORE TO TANNERS HATCH YOUTH HOSTEL

Circular walk—3 miles. Bluebells in spring
Combine with Walk Fifteen for 5 miles+ walk

Maps SSA P 86 5A.
Start in NT East CP (pay and display or display NT card on dash.) on Ranmore Common Road.

Turn left (west) out of CP, cross road and keep walking west.

A hundred yards or so from the CP, you'll come to 3 cottages on your right. After the driveway of the third of these, you'll come to a wooden barrier with a green arrow on the right hand post, along with a green YHA sign.

Take the path left, passing through another wooden barrier, then on along a flat grass and dirt track. The path you're on drops fairly sharply, shortly after a diagonal grassy track intercepts it

Almost at the bottom of the hill you'll pass through another wooden barrier. Here, turn right on to the wide flatish track leading downhill.

This track changes colour slightly to chalk on a slight incline. Keep an eye left for glimpses of Polesden Lacey. As you come to the crest of the track, it curves downward right, then sharply left. You're almost at the youth hostel.

As you catch sight of Tanners Hatch Y H, another wide track runs into yours from the right. Walk on along this even wider track which takes you along side the hostel, with accompanying wooden fence which is it's boundary.

Tanners Hatch, a NT property has been a Y H for over 50 years. The hostel offers simple self catering accommodation, peace and seclusion, plus fine views of Polesden with the closest parking 3/4 of a mile away.

Leaving the hostel behind, the track wends downhill, with an open field left. Looking back over your left shoulder you can see again the grounds of Polesden Lacey but not the house.

In the distance to the right, across open fields lies a large building, Old Dene. As the track curves left, and before it starts an ascent, go through the wide wooden farm gate right. Follow the well walked track across the field, which brings you closer to Old Dene.

This leads you beside Bagden Farm, and you'll pass through two wooden gates only yards apart beside and right of the farm buildings. After the second gate, turn right onto the obvious track which runs uphill. You'll now have a much closer view of Old Dene left.

From here it's a slow easy climb back to Ranmore Common road. Higher up the track enters woodland with carpets of bluebells in places in spring.

As the climb levels out and you walk into a clearing there's a track running off downhill left. Ignore it. The path you're on levels further, a hedge right and in springtime there is a field full of cowslips on the other side.

At the top of this field lies The Rectory, consisting of large and beautiful flint buildings with stone corners. This property lies just off the Ranmore Common road. A few more yards and the track brings you out almost opposite the Ranmore Church, St Barnabas.

Turn right and follow the track through the grass, which widens and cuts a corner keeping you well away from the road and leading directly to the car park. If it's muddy walk along the road instead.

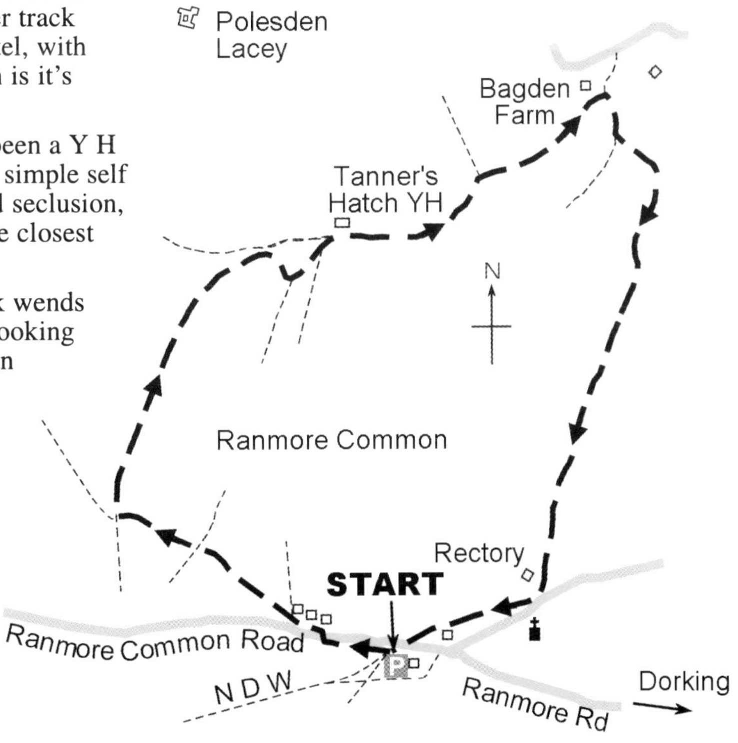

8. ONE WAY TICKET TO RIDE - DORKING TO LEATHERHEAD

Undulating, 6 miles. Scenic train ride.
Some mud but very walkable in wet conditions

Maps SSA P87 D5 OS SSA p115 C1
Start Dorking Railway Station

From main front doors of Dorking station, walk up to A24, cross then turn right up to traffic lights. Cross the entrance of Ashcombe Road still walking beside A24, past Chichester Close and into Chichester Road.

Walk to the Tee junction at the end of the road then turn left up hill. At the corner, look for a wooden footpath post. Follow the arrow, through the wooden gate then up a narrow path, houses left. When you see a road left, you'll also see another footpath sign. This leads you straight on to an obvious generous path through the woods.

At the top of the rise, at a Tee junction turn right on to a wider path which leads you through a kissing gate into Denbies. This is a mucky stretch in wet weather. Keep straight on until you're on to a wide gravel track. There's a footpath post here, with a wide grassy track left, or the gravel track right. Take the left grassy track. You'll see the Denbies buildings right.

At a 4 way junction, with a bitumened track running right, down to the buildings, keep straight on across to the footpath to the left of the fence. Go over a stile on to this narrow path fence right, hedgerow left.

Once over the 2nd stile, you'll find yourself on a wide vehicle track, (NDW). There's a footpath post immediately right. Go straight on, crossing the NDW. You'll soon be walking beside a wooden rail fence left, on a farm track. Stay on this track as it curves right downhill. You can see West Humble right.

Follow this track all the way down to Chapel Lane, passing the remains of the chapel at the bottom, right. Turn left into Chapel Lane, a flint wall right. When the wall ends there's a wide metal gate. Go through this gate into the field (now N T property) and keep to the right fence line, all the way to the stile at the top of the hill. This stretch is mucky when very wet.

Go through the unique wooden stile at the bottom of a power pole, and on up a narrower winding path through the brambles to another stile. Cross into the field. You'll see Crabtree Cottages ahead left. Walk straight on up to the next stile which leads you on to Crabtree Lane. There's an inviting wide wooden seat here.

Turn right along the lane, away from the cottages. Shortly after it becomes a descent you'll reach a CP left. Turn left and walk through the CP continuing on the bridleway. After 4–5 mins maybe less, it joins a wide bitumened path. Continue along it in the same direction.

It's easy walking now, passing a bridleway left and then reaching the Druid's Grove viewpoint right, another opportunity for a break with a birds eye view. Shortly after this you'll reach the saw mill left..

With picnic tables left, and Norbury House right, just ahead you'll see a wide wooden barrier and a narrow wooden gate. Pass through the gate and take the left fork. The first little bit is a bit soggy when wet but most of this wide level path offers easy walking. Follow this track to a junction. Here turn left downhill, a fence and fields right. In wet weather it's best to keep to the narrow path to the left.

About half way down you'll view Leatherhead and Bocketts Farm right. At the bottom of the hill, at the Tee junction, turn right towards the farm. Once again keep to the left edge of the path in wet weather. You may feel the need of a cuppa coming on as you approach the farm. If not, pass the CP left and farm right, continuing more or less straight on up to Young Street.

Cross over to the bridleway which continues through a wooded area for about 1/2 a mile. After this you will come to an open field right. When the field ends turn right downhill following the bridleway. It then runs left on level ground, then right across a railway bridge, and on down a rocky track.

Left you'll soon see the Leisure Centre and right, Thorncroft vineyard. (You are in Thorncroft Drive). Just on from here at a four way junction, turn left, the Leisure Centre still on your left. Walk out along the drive to Waterway Road, then along Waterway Road to the lights.

Don't turn left under railway tunnel. Instead cross at lights and walk on through park to pedestrian lights at other end. Cross and turn left under the railway bridge then right up to ticket office.

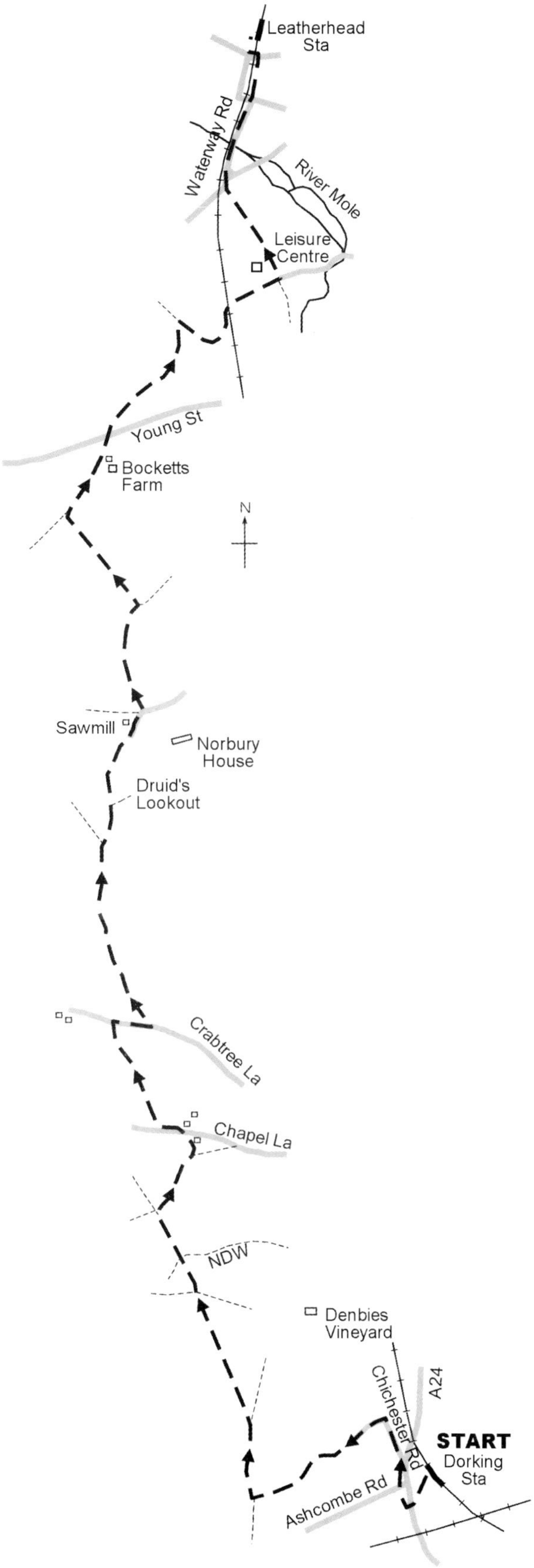

9. HEADLEY HEATH

Some hills, 4 miles

Bluebells and gorse and Highland Cattle

Maps SSA P88 A1 OS SSA p96 C2
Start at the Cock Public House next to Headley Church. (If you plan to have a meal, it's best to walk first.)

Walk away from the Church through the pub car park, past the Village Hall Store, past Dobbes nursery keeping to the footpath at the left side of the road. After a short distance, you'll pass through a metal barrier and a hedge will screen you from the road.

Keep walking with the road always close right. Every now and then you'll view it as you come to a lane entrance or driveway. Just after one of these, you'll walk between a wooden barrier. Then the path will wend between the trees until you come to another wooden barrier and a view of the road again.

Left you will see a sign indicating the entrance of the Manor House. Cross this entrance drive and walk straight along the drive of the White Lodge Headley Cricket grounds. Skirt around the back of the cricket house, then towards Headley Common Road and the NT car park (with the food wagon. Do not be way-laid!)

Cross the road and walk through the middle of the car park heading for the large Headley Heath National Trust sign at the back. Take the path just left of this sign. Once you begin the descent, keep to the right of the gravel track and watch for a path right between wooden posts.

Now head downhill, (still in view of the gravel track) once more following the indistinct grassy path to the bottom of the hill. This is an easier descent than the rough loose gravel track you were on.

At the bottom, join the original wide gravely track left and walk straight on. You will see steps leading up a slope on your left. The track you're on curves left and you will see a wooden post left.

Just after this turn right onto a track marked by a finger post with a blue arrow. This track goes up steeply. Take your time, resting whenever you need. Keep walking up hill until you come to High Ashurst Youth Camp. Walk away from their sign up a long straight sealed track.

After several hundred yards you will reach a cluster of picturesque, beautifully kept buildings named Bellasis, boasting a bell tower, rhododendrons and a walled garden. Walk on a little further to some wide wooden gates left, a National Trust Headley sign and another finger post with a blue arrow.

Concentrate on directions extra carefully from here. Following the blue arrow, stay on this wide track as it winds downhill. Once you start a gentle climb again, this track will soon be dissected by a grassy diagonal path with a metal barrier left. Go straight across, still ascending.

A short while after the path flattens out, passing bluebells left and right, you'll walk into a clearing with 6 or 7 paths intersecting it. Take the second path right (probably the dirtiest track) which is obviously very muddy when wet.

This track curves left and downhill, then heads up hill again. When it curves right almost at the top of the rise, walk straight ahead on to a different track. At a Tee junction and wooden barrier, turn left on to a wide bridleway. Then take the second path you come to on your left.

After about 15–20 paces turn sharp right again onto a footpath that winds more or less parallel to the bridleway you were on. Best to leave the bridleway to the horses. The footpath is more picturesque.

This footpath is not obvious on the O S map. It curves left and right passing some picnic tables left, then silver birches right, and highland cattle left, finally returning you to the NT CP.

From here, once again it's a matter of retracing your steps to the church, or you could start the walk at this carpark, shortening it by a mile or so. Remember to put your NT card on the dash, or pay and display. The fee is very little for the huge beneficial effect the National Trust has on the environment.

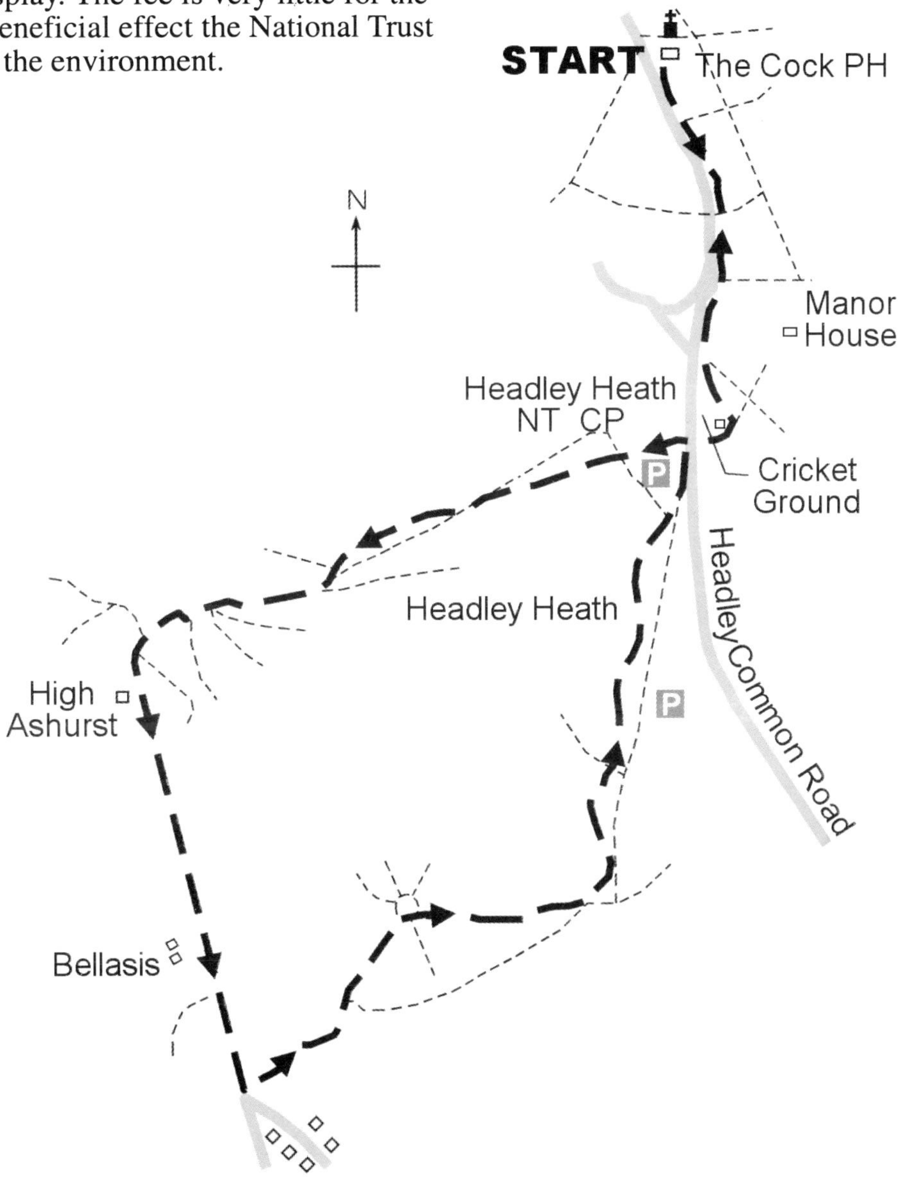

10. BATS, BOX HILL & A LITTLE FOLLY

Hills, 3¼ miles.

Maps SSA Page 87 3D OS SSA p116 C/D8
Start Headley Heath N T C P

A charming, varied walk for all times of year (especially a balmy summer's evening). The easiest route up Box Hill Plenty of shade on a hot summers day, glorious views, masses of wildflowers, blackberries, plenty of interest.

Driving from Mickleham on Old London Road, turn left onto Headley Road. The car park (not marked on the atlas) is about ½ a mile on the right after this junction, on Headley right corner of SSA P 87 3D.

Follow the public bridleway sign along the obvious track which leads away from the road,(start of Juniper Bottom). About 12 paces along this track you'll come to a NT sign board with a map of the area and Box Hill.

Compare this with your mud map and read the contour lines to see where you'll be walking up or down hill and how steep (not very) it will be. If the contour lines are very close together, you know it will be very steep.

Walk further on the same track and after about 20 paces, you'll see a National Trust funds box left. After another 200 yds or so you'll come to a clearing and will see a path leading steeply uphill right. Continue on the track you're on, but remember this point for later.

When the track does begin to climb, you'll scarcely notice it. When you do find yourself obviously climbing, you're almost at the top.

Just after the crest of the hill you'll reach a junction with a path left and right. Ignore both and take the middle path as it veers left. 10–20 paces you'll come to a second junction. In June and July you'll sight a grove of foxgloves along the path on your right. Once again take the middle path.

The climb is over. Now it's a shady walk until you come to a picket fence at the boundary of a mobile home or caravan site. Keep this site left and follow the track to the roadside where you'll look across to Boxhill Tavern

Cross the road and turn right along the footpath to the side of the road. Take the first path left, which will lead you (after 40–50 paces) to another path (out of sight) running parallel to the road. This is part of the North Downs Way. Turn right on to it.

You'll see the acorn symbol for the NDW on finger posts now and then. This path will lead you to clearings left with spectacular views from Kent to Leith Hill to Westcott, encompassing Brockham, Betchworth and Dorking. At the first clearing there's a well placed seat right.

Continue along the NDW following the occasional acorn signs. The path leads on downhill through some trees with many roots making the going a jot precarious. Wet wood is likely to be slippery. and this patch can be very slippery in the winter.

The next clearing (the top of Box Hill), has a trig point (survey marker), marked by a chunky white concrete obelisk, and offers an even finer view.

When you're ready, continue on the same track slightly downhill between the trees. At a gap in the trees left you will glimpse part of Denbies vineyard and Ranmore. The path curves right and slightly uphill.

Left, the NDW path exits down steps rather steeply. Ignore it and keep on more or less flat and straight ahead. As you come to a wooden picket fence right you'll have a view of almost the entire vineyard.

When you reach the crest of the hill another path joins yours, from the right. Carry straight on. You'll catch sight of Norbury House through the next gap in the trees. About 10 paces on from this you'll reach the head stone of an eccentric who was buried here head down in 1800!

Another 40–50 paces on, look for a slightly obscure path right, not far from a well decayed tree stump. This leads off through the brambles). It's a well worn if narrow path.

When you come to a tall wire fence where the path forks, take the left fork and keeping the fence right, follow it round to the old fort. You'll see the red brick building and a large sign with details about the fort and it's current inhabitants.

Walk on up hill on a gravel track, past the National Trust building right until you come to a road. Go straight across following the wooden finger post that indicates public bridleway. This path will quickly bring you into a parking area.

Turn right into the parking area and keep to the left boundary of the car park. Exit from the carpark at the first path you come to left. You'll pass between an earth bank left and a hefty log right. The path then leads you past a clearing on the right with occasional wooden seats.

Keep on the main track as it veers left. Ignore a track running off right. You will find yourself heading very slightly downhill. If you're walking in June or July you will smell the honeysuckle before you see it.

You'll see a wooden post left, with a blue horseshoe, a black oak symbol and a blue arrow. Keep to the left track. Another 50 paces or so, you'll spot a low wooden sign left saying 'no bicycles'.

It's all down hill from here. The path you're on is wide and well surfaced, and feels like it will go on for ever. From time to time you will see a blue arrow.

You will see Westhumble on your left through a clearing in the trees, and a little further on, Box Hill and Dorking. About 50 yards further on from this last view you will come to a folly, with a tree growing up through it. Juniper Hall, the Surrey Wildlife Educational Trust Centre, lies directly below you and in the distance are Norbury House and Norbury Park.

After taking in the view, turn right then follow the path which soon curves down hill left. At a junction with 2 wooden finger posts, take the right path. At the next junction take the left path downhill. This path will become quite steep. You'll finally come to steps for the last part of the descent. These will bring you to the clearing you noted at the beginning of the walk. Once you reach the track, turn left and it's a couple of hundred yards to the car park.

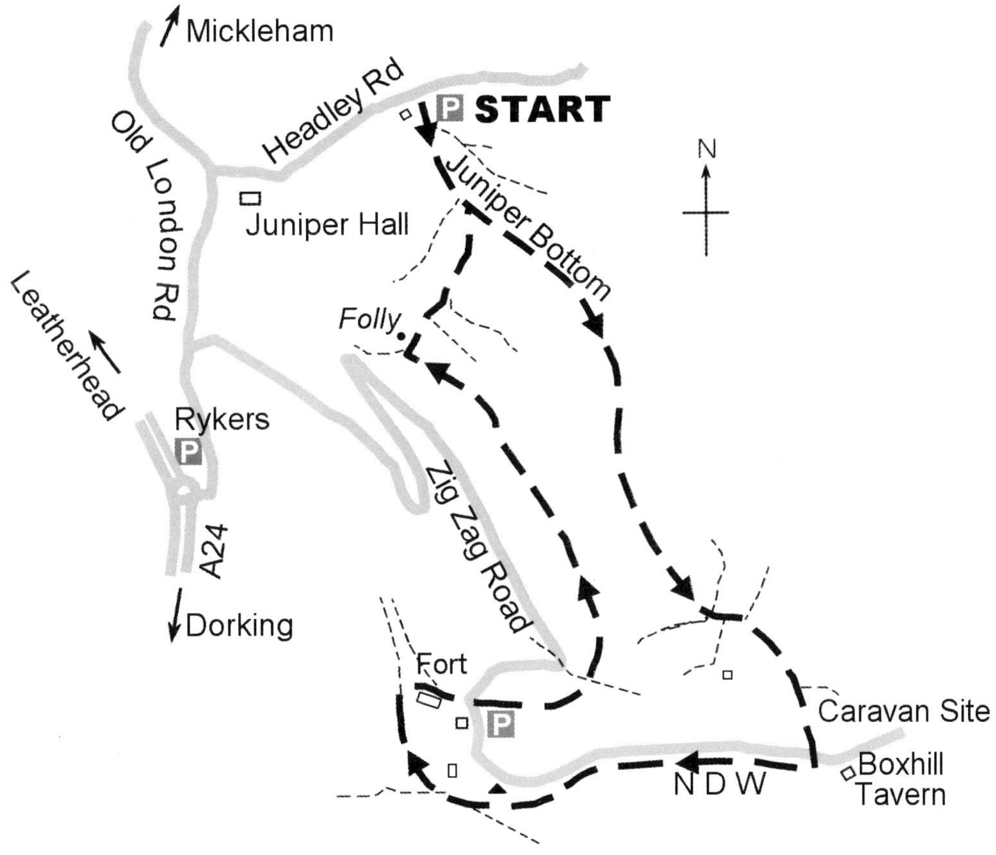

11. NOOKS AND CRANNIES OF NORBURY

Undulating, 4+ miles

Maps SSA page 87, D4. OS SSA p115 C1 **Start** at the small car park at West Humble Station. There don't appear to be any parking restrictions or fees here, but check with the station master if walking during the day. **Start at** Ryka's CP at Burford Bridge for 5 miles +.

Climb the steps which lead from the car park to the road. Cross the road and turn left along the railway bridge. Immediately the bridge ends, you will see a footpath sign pointing right to a path along side the railway line.

After passing through a small wooden gate walk up to the left side of the large field you are in. The track through the grass is faint at first but as you reach some steps with a wooden handrail left, it becomes quite distinct. A few yards past the steps you'll see a sign which says Pickering Plantation etc. Ten to fifteen paces further is a wooden seat, but you won't be ready for it yet.

Follow the worn track to a large wooden gate, and go through. This brings you to woods and a gentle incline, which becomes steeper. At the top of the rise you'll see the corner of a field and another large gate.

Take the track immediately left of the gate and field, still walking through woods and again climbing slightly, with the fence right. You may glimpse Norbury House through the trees, on the skyline.

This path quickly brings you to a wide flat track running left and right. Turn right, and keeping a sharp eye left, walk about 50 yards until you see a narrow path leading left up hill. Follow this narrow path which, after a few paces swings right.

For a while it's very easy walking, as the path winds gently uphill. Again you'll see Norbury House on the skyline, much closer. The path steepens, but not for long. Just as it levels out, you may notice some slightly over grown steps left, which would take you up to a higher path which runs more or less parallel with the one you're on.

However ignore them for now. It's easy walking and level for quite a way (apart from a few tree roots). After this long flattish patch, there's a definite downhill stretch. Then, as the path starts to climb again, there's another track running downhill fairly steeply right. Ignore it, and walk on another 50 paces or so.

You'll come to a fork and will see steps up the path left. Climb these, that lead, zigzagging, to Druids Grove Lookout. You'll have views of Mickleham. and a welcome seat.

Continue on from here uphill to the left of the seat, to the picnic tables, then on to a wide path. At the fork (a matter of 10 or so paces), take the right path and when you reach the narrow sealed road, turn right again on to it. You'll soon come to the boundary fence of Norbury House.

Keep on this road as it winds round and down past the house. Pass the main gate and turn right on to a footpath just before a wooden seat. The boundary fence will still be on your right.

When you reach the rear gate of Norbury House, turn your back on it and head down hill. This path swings right, giving you a clear view of Mickleham.

At a corner where the road turns left downhill, you'll see a wooden finger post. Take the path to the right at this sign which takes you into shrubby woodland. This is now part of The Mole Gap Art Walk. Keep your eyes peeled for the Art. Walk along this path until you see a wooden gate and path left which indicate Swanworth Farm picnic area.

At the other end of the picnic ground pass though an identical gate and walk straight ahead along a dirt farm track. This brings you to the farm house on your left (Lodge Farm). Turn left through a small wooden gate after the farm buildings then right onto the gravel farm track which takes you across the humped bridge.

After a right angle bend to the left you will reach Cowslip Farm. Keep to the right of the farm and turn right on to a track running under power lines. This track will lead you past another house right.

Pass though the wooden gate into the field and walk straight on, coming to another wooden gate. There's a fence right now and the path will lead you across a low wooden bridge beside an arched railway bridge (worth a close look).

Once over the bridge you're now in the same field in which you started. Keeping to the left near the railway line, with power lines 10–20 yards to your right, you will soon find yourself back at the first wooden gate and West Humble Station.

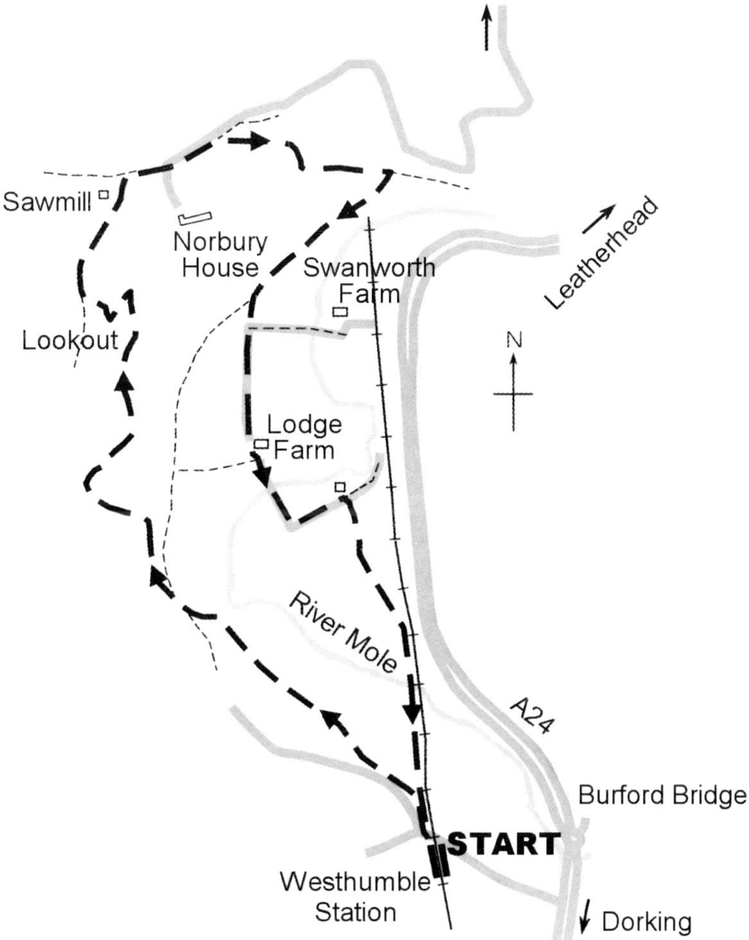

12. SOUTH OF WESTCOTT

Easy, undulating, 4 miles.

Maps SSA Page 105 D2 OS SSA p135 B5

Start at The Holy Trinity Church, (off A25) in Logmore Lane at Westcott. (Parking restricted Sundays.)

Walk down hill and turn right into Heath Rise, (before the cottages). At the end of Heath Rise is a footpath running left and right. Turn left, walk 40–50 paces then take the first footpath on your right which runs between houses and gardens.

When you come to a road go straight across, where the footpath continues. You'll soon have fields on either side, beyond the immediate boundary fences.

The first farm you reach on your left is Applegarth. At a road 50–100 yds on from the farmhouse go straight on. You'll have open hillside right and trees immediately left.

When you reach another junction with a farm track coming in diagonally from the left, keep going straight ahead, onto another farm track. left of straight ahead. When you reach the next road, turn left for 10–20 paces and walk to the corner of a field bedecked with signs, Logmore Farm, April Cottage, Brook Farm etc.

Don't turn right down dirt lane (unless you want a short cut). Cross the stile into the field, following the sign that says Public Footpath. Head for the diagonally opposite corner of the field. There may be horses which will take little interest in you. (Never feed any farm animals.)

You'll see wooden farm buildings beyond the fence on the left. There's a well worn track through the grass in places. Keep to the left side of the field and you'll find the next stile to cross in the left corner to the left of a pond.

Once over the stile, you'll see marsh grasses and occasionally water right, with an accompanying wooden fence left. At the end of this short section, is a third stile to climb over. Cross the stream and again walk diagonally across this field. At time of writing there's no worn path across this field.

Look along the left fence line. You'll see electricity wires running from a pole on the left. About 50 yards to the right of this pole you'll see a yellow footpath arrow on another wooden stile. Climb over this and keep to the right fence. This will lead you to a corner of the field, another stile and Squires farm.

Turn right between the house and the farm buildings then follow the track round to the left of the property. There may be two noisy dogs here, but they're on the other side of a sturdy 5 foot fence.

This path leads you in to a mostly pine forest. The track is wide and the atmosphere quite different. At the first junction turn right up hill. It's sandy soil with lots of rocks so mind your step. Almost at the top of the hill, you'll come to a five way junction. Go straight across. The slope is very slight now.

Ignore the first track on your right. The flora changes here and on top of the hill the path is level for some distance. When you come to the next junction, turn right along Wolvens Lane (not signed). As it's a byway you could meet the occasional vehicle.

The walk continues along the top of this ridge for a mile and a bit now and can be very mucky in wet weather. You will pass a memorial stone on your right, in memory of two Kingston Ramblers. There's a short downhill stretch after this (not steep). Then you'll see a wooden footpath sign in the middle. Keep straight on.

When the path levels again you have the option of a path with views on your left, running along the fence line, and parallel to the track you're on.

A little further on as you view the North Downs on the skyline the 4WD track will become two. Take the left. You'll pass a wooden Public Bridleway sign in the middle of these two tracks, and just after it you'll have a gentle descent.

Keep an eye out to the left. You'll shortly glimpse some low farm buildings beyond an open field. Now watch on your right for another wooden footpath sign pointing right to a downhill track. This is not very steep but once again can be very muddy if wet.

Take this downhill path which leads past ponds right. It eventually will lead you to Rookery Hill Farm, a beauty spot at any time of year. After passing between the 2 picturesque cottages, follow their driveway back to the A25.

From here, follow the path right up hill to Westcott Heath. When you reach the top of the hill walk across the flat, keeping parallel but to the left of the road and houses. You can either follow the road back to your car, or turn left, just as you start downhill, through the church yard gate, and admire the church as you go.

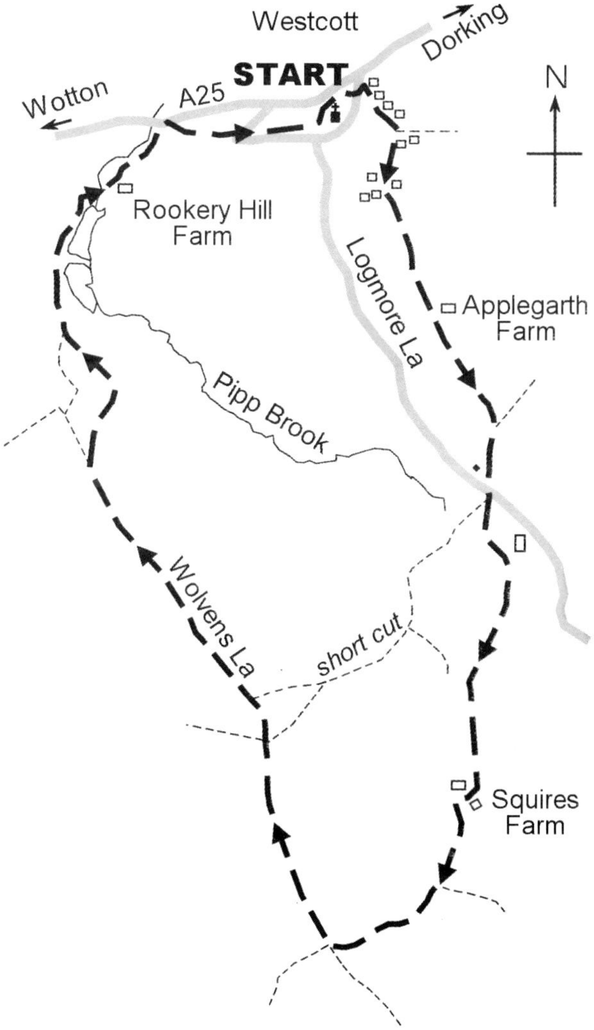

13. RANMORE & PILGRIMS WAY

Easy, undulating, 4 miles – one climb.
Lovely walk for spring wild flowers

Maps SSA Page 86 5A OS SSA p114 C1
Start at Ranmore east NT CP (pay and display or display NT card on dash). Little or no public transport.

Turn your back on the road and go through the wooden gate, or over the stile beside it. Stay in the field, walking diagonally right down over the brow of the hill. (Don't take the path to the gate on your extreme right.)

You'll soon see a distinct path through the grass. Follow it to another wooden gate and pass down through it. Turn right and with wonderful views over Westcott and farmlands, walk along the highest well worn path that runs just below the fence line. (You will also see a track not so far below you. Later you will be walking along this track.)

When you reach the corner of the fence on your right you'll see a wider path with a slight but comfortable downhill slope (just about room for 2 abreast) which takes you under a huge Yew tree. There are a few rabbit holes, and sometimes wild ponies. Never feed them.

This finally brings you to a gate when you're almost at the bottom of the hill. Go through this gate and into the woods. Walk about 50 yards, keeping an eye on the fence line on your left for a gate.

Pass through this gate and look for a vague path which runs slightly diagonally left downhill. It then zig zags a few feet, before running straight on down hill to the level wide track seen earlier. (It's only 20–30 yards from the gate to this track). Turn left along it.

Fifty yards or so on, you'll come to a wide wooden gate. Go through it. Twenty or so paces further, you'll come to a new track that has a hairpin bend in it. Turn left on to this new well surfaced dirt track. You'll be walking slightly up hill for a minute or two passing very tall trees and wild flowers in season. (You'll be walking to the end of this track, about 1 and 1/4 miles 30–40 mins for most)

Continue along this path as it climbs almost unnoticeably. You'll enter a patch of Yews and see a steep path up hill left which would return you to the car park if you wanted to.

Entering another patch of yews there's a wide path on your left disappearing round a bend. This only leads to the road. Keep on the path you're on which soon becomes a definite but gentle descent.

This track eventually leads you to a wide metal gate. About 20 yards before this gate look for a path to your right running downhill through the woods. Mind your step. There are many tree roots.

Follow this path through this small area of woods until you come to a T junction. Turn left uphill, the picket fence right. This will bring you to the road, and you now have a short stretch of easy roadside walking uphill. The foot path is left of the road, mostly about six foot above road level.

It's an easy climb up to a wooden finger post on the right. You'll see a path across the road and a stone wall to the left of this path. Cross the road and walk up this narrow path, between two fences. Once again, it's an easy climb, if a little overgrown at times.

When you reach a junction there may be deer in the field left. Keep on up hill. You'll pass another field right, as the track becomes level. This also often holds deer. (Don't take the path downhill right.)

Opposite this field lies a white cottage.

At the corner of the cottage, turn left. It's fairly level walking from here, and you're on the NDW again. Fifty yards or so, you'll come to the corner of a sealed road.

Heading in the same direction, walk on the grass left of the road.

you reach the church, St Barnabas, cross over. Follow a track through the grass and into the trees. This track widens and cuts a corner keeping you away from

the road and leading directly to the car park. However, this short cut is very mucky if it's wet. If so it's easier to stay by the road and follow it to Ranmore Common Road. Turn right and you'll see the CP.

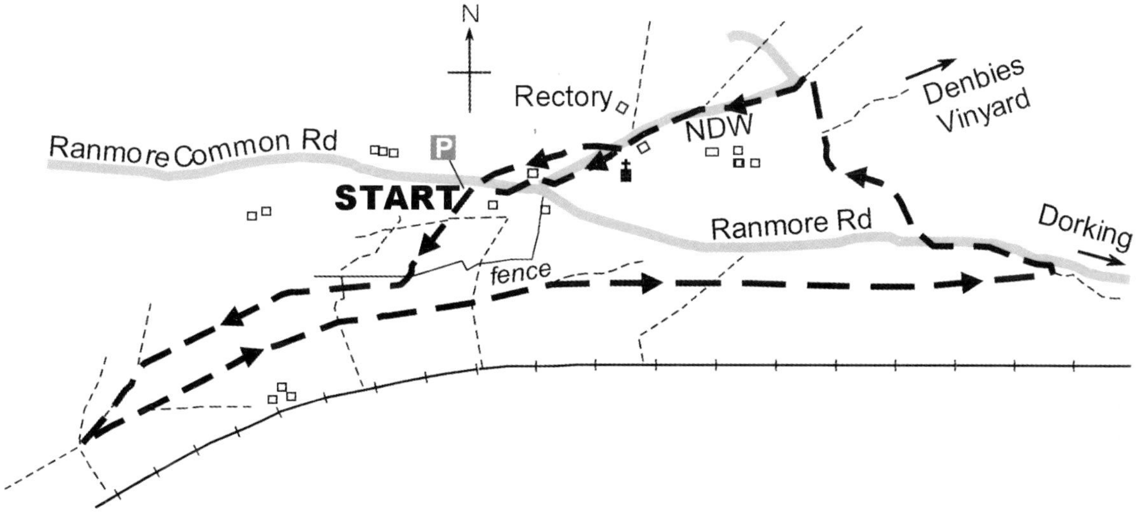

14. BOCKETTS FARM TO CRABTREE COTTAGES

Easy, undulating, 4½ miles.

Maps SSA P86 B1 OS SSA p94 F2
Park in the Bocketts Farm car park next to the farm. (Or there is a CP at the Young Street top roundabout or it's 25 min walk from Leatherhead centre.)

Standing in the drive with the tea room and shop on your left and the animal barns and pond right, walk straight ahead on the middle farm track as it winds up and round to the left. Stay on this track, keeping the fence left beside you all the way to a wide wooden gate. Climb over the stile right of this gate. You'll have views across to Givons Grove and Tyrrell's Wood.

Walk another 40–50 paces with the fence line close left, then as soon as you're able, turn right into the grassy field keeping fairly close to the right fence line and hedge. A well worn path soon becomes evident.

Walk the full length of the field to the corner, by the railway line. Turn into the field right, that runs above the railway track. The gate may be open here or use stile. Leave gate as you find it.

Keep close to the trees and boundary fence left until you're near the far end of the field. Here veer right and uphill a jot. You'll soon see a wide gate and stile. Head for those. and cross.

Walk straight on down hill. At the junction of paths at the bottom, turn right and follow this path as it climbs gently, eventually bringing you to the road to Norbury House. Turn right up the road, still climbing for 5 minutes or so.

You'll soon pass Norbury House left. Keep straight on. At the junction, pass the picnic tables and wood mill right. (There's a wooden barrier as you reach the mill).

When the boundary fence left ends, you'll reach a viewpoint sign another 50 or so paces on. This slight detour to your left is the perfect opportunity to relax on the generous wooden seat, whilst enjoying the view across to Mickleham, Juniper Tops and Box Hill.

When ready, return to the road and carry on, over the speed bump, and more or less straight ahead.

As the path starts to slope very noticeably downhill, curving to the left, you'll find yourself face to face with an uphill track. There's a tall wooden finger post on the left side and a short wooden post saying 'bicycles' on the right)

Leave the track you're on and take this new track following it to the CP at it's end, then onto Crab Tree Lane. Turn right up Crab Tree Lane and follow the lane to the cottages. Turn right at the cottages keeping to the main wide track. Parts of this track are very mucky when wet.

Follow this track for some time. You'll notice two large power pylons, on your right, then the line crosses to your left and out of sight.

When this path eventually forks, take the right fork. Walk about 20 paces to the wooden barrier to the right of the path. Pass through barrier and walk straight ahead to the first path on your left. (Not far) Turn left here. This is a beautiful leafy stretch, and good underfoot.

At the T junction, walk straight across the first track and turn left onto the second (which runs parallel with the first that you crossed). After about 20 paces this brings you to a wooden barrier. Go through this barrier and across to and through the next wooden barrier.

This leads you downhill through a high leafy tunnel. There's light at the end of the tunnel, and a junction, with a huge beech left and a wooden seat beneath it.

Here you have 2 options. You can walk straight ahead and up the wide gravel track as it curves right. When you reach the top of the hill you will see Bocketts farm below you to the right. If it's very wet, this route is the driest underfoot.

Or you can turn right—not the first track sharp right, but the second track which leads gently down hill, passing a farm building right. Just after this building you'll see a track leading off up to the right, which then turns left and runs parallel to the track you've just left and is good underfoot. When this ends veer left again onto the main path, and carry on to the farm.

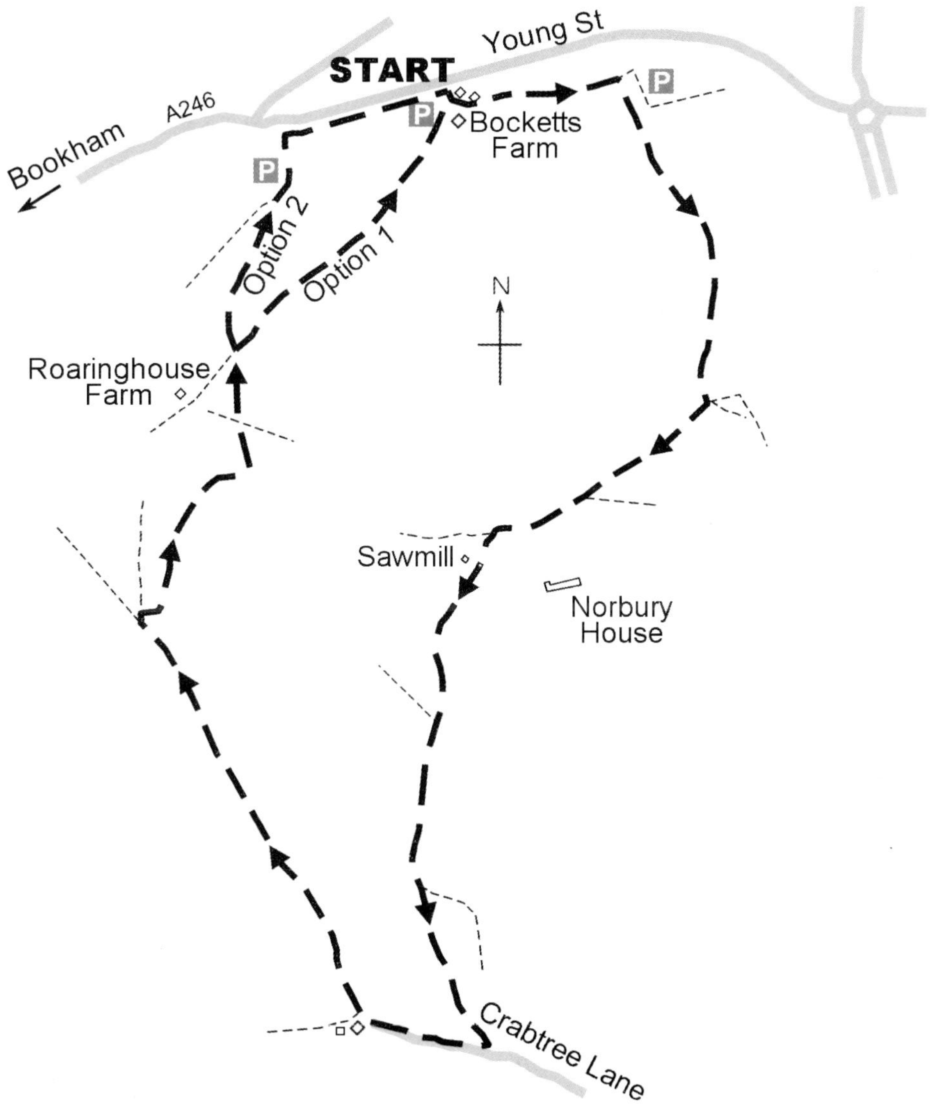

15. POLESDEN LACEY, RANMORE & THE NORTH DOWNS WAY

Easy, undulating, 4½ miles.

Maps SSA Page 86 5A. OS SSA p114 C1
Start at Ranmore east National Trust car park.
(pay and display or display NT card on dash.)
Combine with walk 7 for longer walk

Go through the wooden gate next to the pay and display. Turn right and walk diagonally on the flat across the field, to double and single wooden gates. You'll see the acorn sign denoting the North Downs Way, on a gate post. Go through this gate and continue, on the flat, straight on. (Ignore the downhill path immediately left.)

This is easy walking on a wide path with sweeping views left. At a first diagonally intersecting path, continue straight on across it. Watch for the acorn. After crossing this diagonal path you'll have yew trees right and beeches left. You'll soon pass a wide mud track going uphill right.

At the next intersection where another path intersects yours, disappearing steeply downhill left, turn right up an easy slope, which soon flattens out.

This path curves right, then back to the left. As it swings left or right. Cross it, walking past a couple of piles of logs left. You're now descending ever so slightly.

Just after this track turns a corner right, you'll see a wooden barrier ahead of you just before the sealed road. (Ranmore Common Road) There's another N T car park at this point, on your right just before the road. (This is an equally good place to begin the walk.)

Go straight across Ranmore Common Road, and walk between the two wooden posts, both with blue arrows. About 10 paces after these 2 posts, you'll come to another post with 3 options. Ignore left and right options and continue on more or less straight ahead. It is a fairly winding, extremely wide path for a while now, and is likely to be very muddy in wet weather, grassy in the summer.

As this track winds more noticeably down hill, the path takes a sharp turn left at another blue arrow. Standing and looking in the direction of this left turn, you'll see a large house ahead and across from you on top of a hill.

Follow the path around to the left and down to a rough farm track (Hogden Lane/ Track). If you look back up this farm track you'll see Pigden Cottage, a beautiful old property. Turn right down hill.

Continue for some time now down this stony track. Mind your ankles. When the stone wall left ends, you'll reach the corner of an open field right with a wooden finger post and stile. Ignore this one. At the bottom corner of a second and adjoining field right, (just after passing a metal pole with a yellow hat right), go through the kissing gate into this field. Walk up the path to a second wooden gate.

As soon as you go through this second gate you'll come on to a path. Cross and pass through a 3rd wooden gate into an open field.

Walk near the fence right and enjoy the superb views left of Polesden Lacey. At the far end of the field turn right through the double gate at the corner. This is Yewtree Farm. Turn left down hill, with a split rail fence right. You'll have wide open views on all sides. Stay on this well surfaced dirt road as it twists downhill to Polesden Farm on the valley bottom.

Instead of walking past the farm, stop while it's still lying straight ahead of you and turn to the 2 gates right. On one gate post, there's a YHA sign and on the other a sign saying Prospect Lodge. Go through the narrower gate and walk up hill with your back to Polesden. It's an easy climb for 5–10 minutes now, but not steep.

At the top of this field, pass through another wooden gate and turn left before reaching the cottage, on to a path running downhill. This undulating path (slippery when wet) will wind through the trees and bring you to Tanners Hatch Youth Hostel.

At the hostel, turn right up the wide well surfaced track until you reach Ranmore Common Road again. Turn left along the side of the road back to the car park.

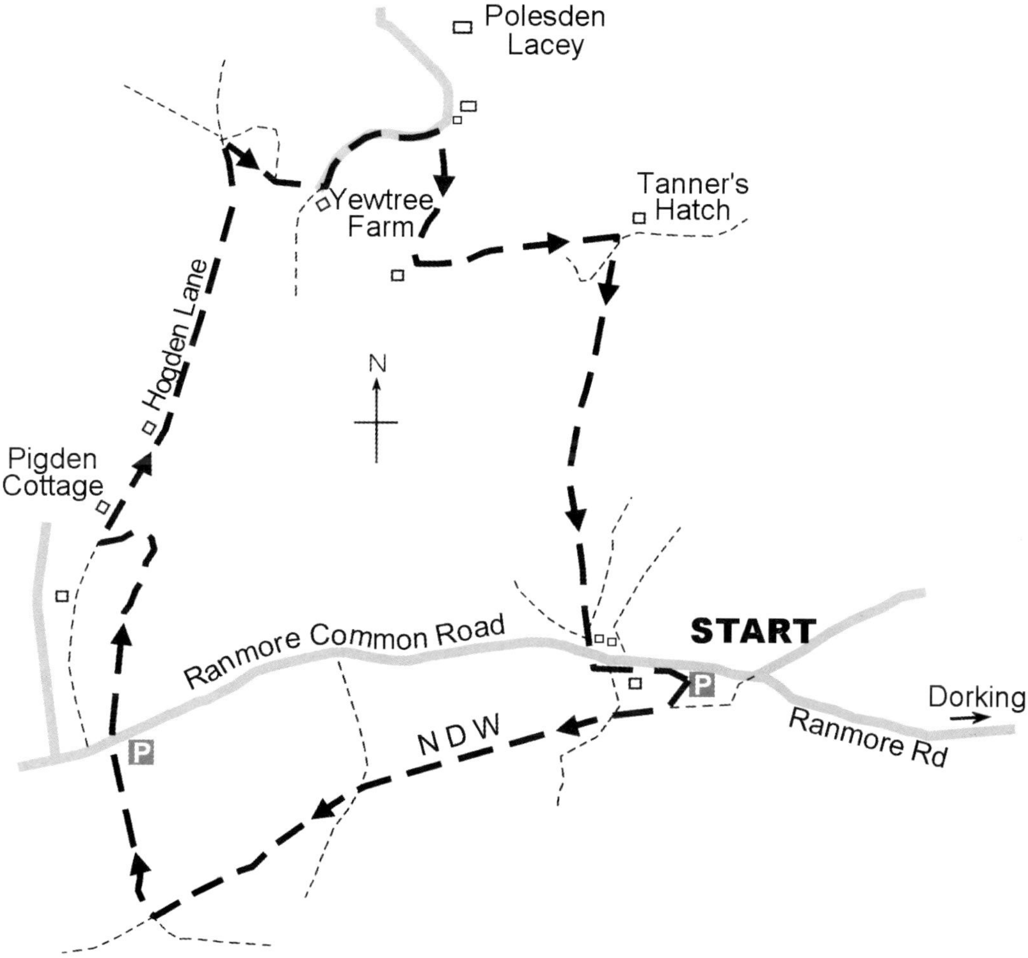

16. EFFINGHAM PONDS

Easy, flat, 4½ miles.

A glorious walk, especially for winter, as there is so much of interest. Very mucky in places—walking boots or wellies.

Maps SSA P85 E2 OS SSA p113 D8
Start at intersection of The Street and Yew Tree Walk. There is limited street parking in The Street near the shops.

Turning your back to the church, walk into Yew Tree Walk, following the tall wooden finger post, (where the shops end. This also leads to The Barn.)

When you reach a red brick wall left and an open field right, go through the stile on your right into the field. Follow the diagonal path across the field to the wooden stile in the far corner and cross.

The path continues between 2 wire fences, still in the same direction. You'll see some houses right, a field left. Duck under a metal barrier and continue. The path finally emerges at Orestan Lane. Turn left and walk along this quiet lane to its end.

Continue straight on up the muddy footpath/ bridleway. (You'll see a wooden finger post.) This track climbs gently for a short distance with a wooden rail fence left, and trees either side, and Great Ridings Wood right, (owned by the Woodlands Trust.)

As the path levels out you'll see a wide wooden gate ahead at a T junction. Turn right on to Old London Road/ Track. This is just one of many old tracks in Surrey which give us an idea of travel in days gone by.

The track descends gently, an old stone wall left (missing or tumbledown in places). When the path forks keep to right fork, (more or less straight on) a ditch either side. There's a tall wooden finger post at this junction).

The track finally comes out on to the end of Heath View private road. Cross the road towards the sign, keeping right of the sign and walk into the corner of the field. Keep to the left edge of the field, a line of houses left .

When you're almost at the woods at the end of the field, turn right, keeping the woods left, and walking away from the houses.

Follow the well worn path as it curves left, then right. At the fork, go straight on (the right fork). On your left now, there' a narrow band of gorse and trees. Keep more or less straight on following this path into the left corner of the field. Continue straight on along the path, out of field. You'll come to a red brick house left, then the path runs into a bitumened farm track. Turn left onto this track, passing a small pond right.

Walk past two properties right. You'll then come to a cricket ground left and a short wooden signpost with yellow arrows.

Turn right just past this post into what looks like a private drive. It leads to a cluster of houses. Once you've turned into this drive, look carefully to your left for a grassy track which leads along the side of a tall hedge and passes left of the dark wooden house.

This brings you to Effingham Common Road. You'll see the entrance of Lower Farm Road on the other side of this road. Cross and walk down this private road to the end.

Climb over the metal stile and turn right along fence line. As you walk, keep your eyes left looking for a large fenced tree. Just beyond it you'll see the ponds (especially in winter) and a wooden stile just to the right of it.

*From here on, concentrate very carefully on the directions, as once you've crossed and passed the ponds, there's a feeling of being in the middle of nowhere.

Cross this wooden vee stile. The path leads across the first pond, where you may be greeted by a bevy of wild fowl.

Leaving this first pond behind, you'll come to a track running left and right. Turn left for 5–10 paces, then turn right, (crossing a stile into a field) just before a sign that says 'Private Land'. Follow the finger post arrow crossing diagonally left to the next pond. Keeping the pond left, follow the fence line to next stile.

Cross and keep walking in the direction of the fence left. You'll see a wide dark green gate ahead at the end of the field, with a stile on its left. Cross, and the track winds right to a second green gate and stile.

Step over this stile once again and veer slightly left. As you reach the middle of the field, you'll see a gap in the trees left. Ignore it and walk straight on to the corner of the field and another vee stile. Cross, and you'll reach two more stiles in quick succession. The last brings you out beside a yellow arrow by another dark green gate.

Walk along this wide pebble farm track as it winds left, then right, a field and barb wire fence right. Then part way along a straight stretch, you'll come to a wooden rail fence left and a PRIVATE sign. Keep straight on, (the pebbles end here) passing a small hut on left immediately after the wooden rail.

You'll glimpse houses and Little Bookham left. After a short distance you'll come to some houses next to the path left and a metal ladder stile beside a wide gate. Climb over, then walk 20 or so paces looking for a track to the right, just opposite the drive of Barn and Farm cottages.

Take this track to the right. There's a hedge and wooden picket fence left and green-houses right. Follow the path to Lower road.

Cross the road and take 10 paces right to the wooden sign post beside stile. Cross stile and walk straight on 20 paces or so to lightly wooded area. Move a few feet to the right here as original path is obstructed. You'll see the school right. Follow the worn path. After 20 or so paces you'll come to a T junction. Turn right and take the right hand path with the back boundary of the school close right.

When you come to the final corner of their boundary keep straight on in the same direction, keeping the flint wall immediately right. This will lead you into the church yard. Cross left behind the church and out in to Church St. Walk straight across into Crossways which links Browns Rd and the Street, and you're back where you started.

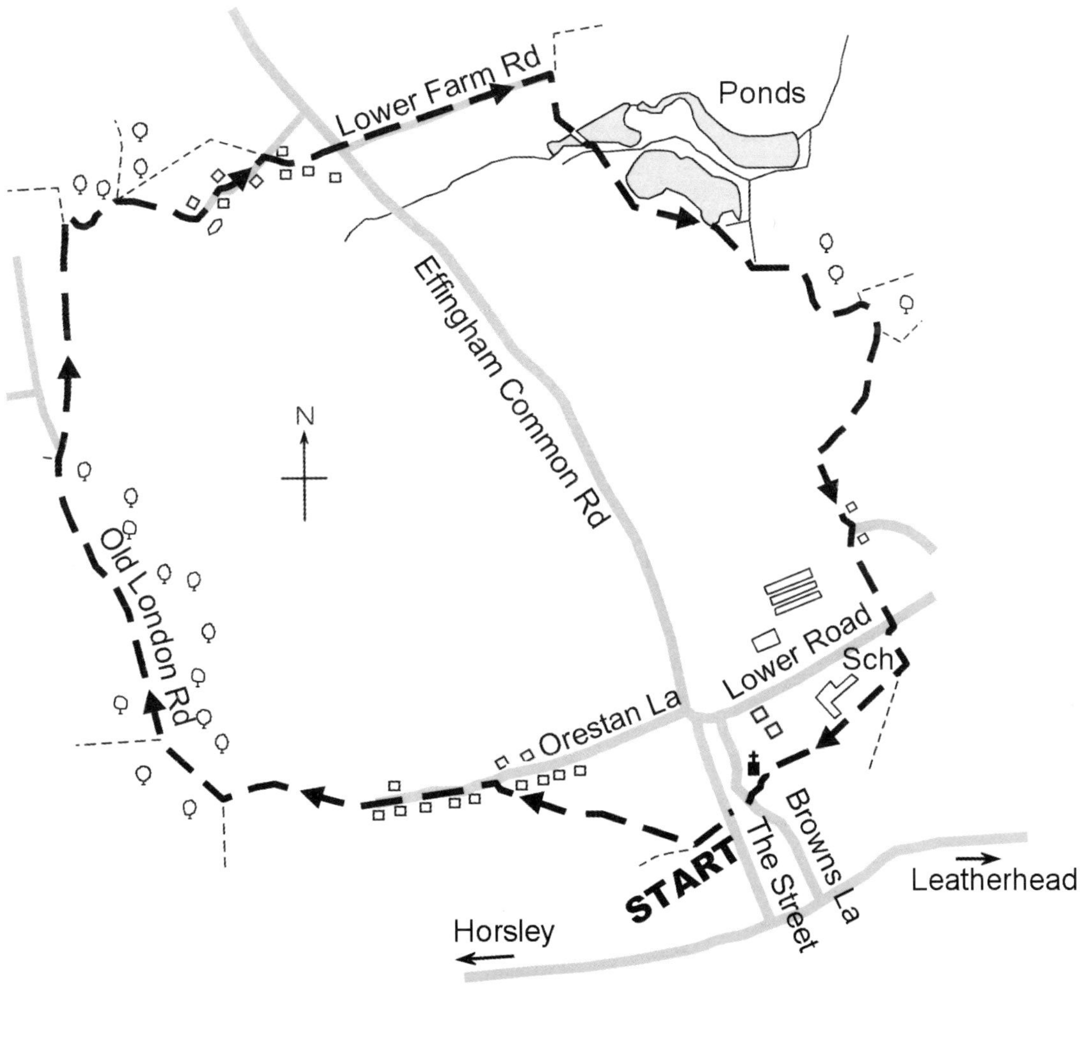

17. FRIDAY STREET TO LEITH HILL

Easy, undulating, 4 ½ miles

Maps SSA P104 C5 OS SSA p155 F8
Start Friday Street CP

If you're driving along the A25 from Dorking, drive through Westcott and Wotton, then turn left into Hollow Lane. Drive down this lane about 2 miles then turn left into Friday Street (a hairpin turn). Drive along here about ¼ mile and just at the crest of a hill, you'll see a large car park right. There is a Tillingbourne bus service which travels down Hollow Lane, which might drop walkers at the entrance of Friday Street. This would add a mile or so.

From the car park, walking parallel with the road, and the road close left, take the track which wends downhill to the pond and Friday Street. Turn right along the sealed lane in front of the pond. Walk the full length of this lane past houses and The Stephan Langton Pub.

Continue straight on as the lane becomes a bridleway, with a tiny stream left. Continue more or less straight on for some distance.

Just after a wooden footbridge left, the path joins a sealed lane (Abinger Common Road). At the fork, keep straight on past some houses. The last on your right is Woodlands.

Continue on this path for the next half mile or so until it forks again. Take the right fork. This quickly brings you to a sealed road. Cross to the path which continues on the other side. (You'll see houses down left.) This brings you to a second road within minutes (Leith Hill Road). Turn left and walk along the side of the road to the brow of the hill for 20–30 yards.

Ignore the Road to Broadmoor. Turn left onto the footpath after the wide wooden barrier. You'll pass a 'DANGER—Fire Hazard' sign right.

Now keep on more or less straight ahead again, easily but steadily climbing, and ignoring any paths that intersect yours.

At a level patch, the path forks. Take the right fork. Here, in winter and early spring, you can see Leith Hill Tower through the trees. After 20–30 paces your path joins a wide track running left to right. Turn left to the tower.

If you're game to climb the tower for splendid views north and south, it's inexpensive and free to NT members.

The views are superb whether you climb the tower or not, looking south to Ockley and north to Ranmore.

When you're ready, walk down the other side of the hill, passing signs left saying Cold Harbour circular walk and Landslip Car Park. Follow this steepish descent to the lowest point, where many tracks merge.

There's a wide wooden barrier left with a light blue arrow pointing north and downhill. Turn left down this bridleway. When you reach a junction with an old wooden seat left, and a diagonally intersecting track, ignore it and continue straight ahead.

At another wide wooden access gate, with a farm right, your path will merge onto a farm track. Pass Pond Cottage right, and your path will emerge at Triple Bar Riding Centre.

Turn left up a sealed track passing houses right. Turn right immediately after Leith Cottage, following the PF sign. This path takes you round to the right behind the houses. When it forks, take the left fork and keep on uphill with your back to the houses .

At the next junction turn left still climbing slightly. As the path levels out you'll reach a sealed lane. Cross over, continue another 100 yds or so and cross a second sealed road.

Now follow the path downhill keeping to the right as it steepens. This brings you out at the Friday Street pond where you started. Retrace your steps up the hill to the car park.

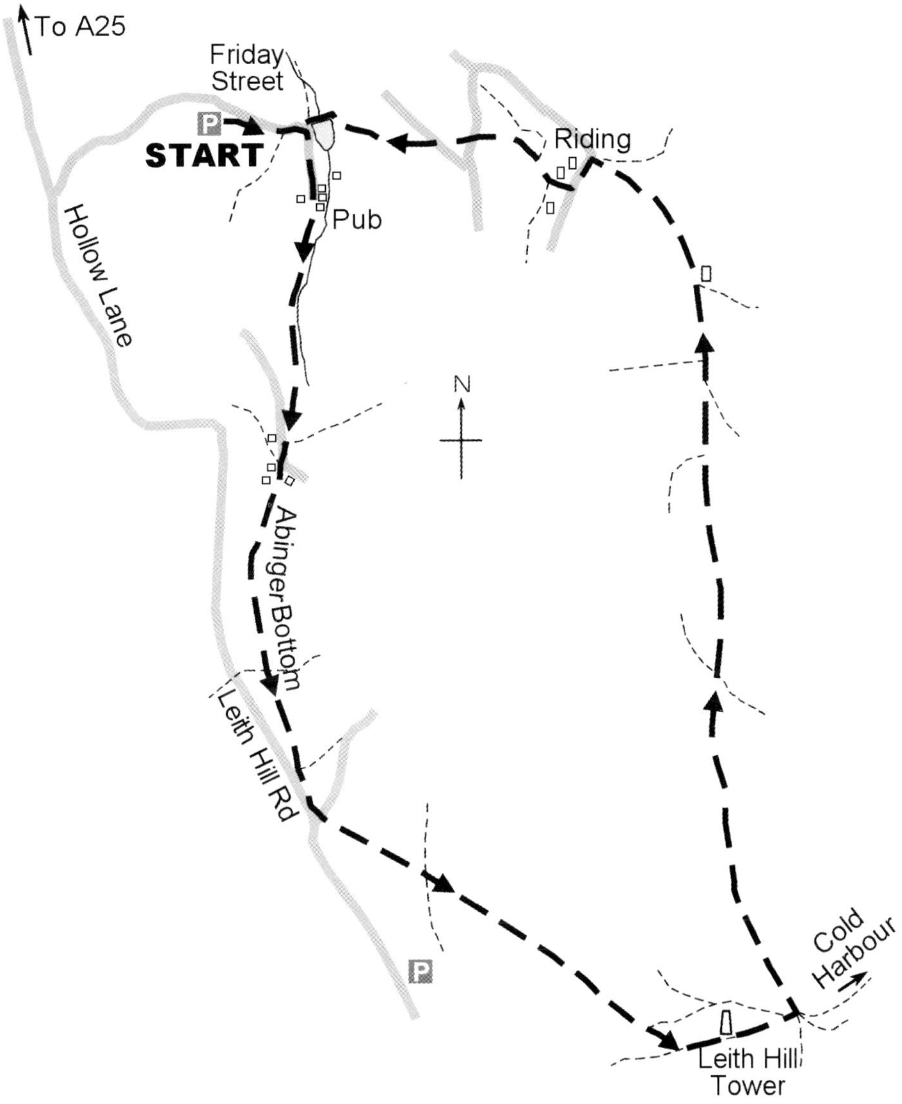

18. MILTON HEATH & WESTCOTT

Easy, 2½ miles

Maps SSA P105 E2 OS SSA p135 E6
Start at Milton Heath CP

From Dorking drive west on A25. Just out of Dorking follow sign on left, 'Bury Hill Fisheries'. Once you've turned left off the A25, ignore CP immediately right by A25 and drive 100 yards or so to the large bumpy parking area (signed CAR PARK) first left.

At the far side of the CP (furthest from road) you'll see the start of a footpath between 2 short stumpy posts. As soon as you've passed between these turn right onto the dirt road/track passing a cottage left. Keep straight on until you come to the main road (A25)

Cross into Milton Court, which is almost opposite the footpath. There's a small stream on the left side of Milton Court Road. The stream leads you to a lake. Walk to the far end of the lake and at the gate house turn left over the bridge. There are some cottages right and a couple of new barn like dark wood buildings.

Once over the bridge turn left. This takes you towards large storage buildings. Keep left of these. Level with the end of these buildings pass through a kissing gate right, which leads you into a field with views up to Ranmore.

Follow the well worn path across the grass. At the far boundary fence, cross the stile into the next field. At this point there's a cottage on your left with a prominent wooden bridge. Keep on more or less straight ahead and cross a 2nd stile at the end of this second field.

At the next (3rd), more civilised 2-step stile you'll see Westcott left. Keep on with the stream left until the path takes you across it into the back streets on the west edge of Westcott.

Cross the sealed road and you'll see the footpath continues on the other side, with a playground right. For more pleasant walking you could follow the playground sign and keeping parallel with the footpath (see map) walk up the left edge of the playing field. At the end of the field turn left back on to the FP.

A few minutes after this you'll emerge at the A25 once again. You'll see some shops to your left. Cross and turn left for 10 yards or so. Turn right into Stones Lane, following the old green footpath sign. This will be the first incline, leading past cottages.

At the Tee junction, turn left. Follow this path at the back of houses. (It could be called Blossom Walk in spring). You'll have views towards Leith Hill to the right, and as you start to descend, views left towards Box Hill. It's tantalising if you're unable to see over the fences to admire the gardens.

A short picket fence eventually replaces the taller fences on a flat stretch of path. Then the path descends once more and leads you past a brick house on your left, across a footbridge onto a narrow sealed road (Milton Street).

Turn right along this quiet back road and keep an eye out for an easy path on your left. Turn left up this path, passing a sandstone cottage on your right. Veer right after this cottage and pass through the wide white gate.

This brings you on to a narrow sealed road. Turn left on this road downhill. As the road curves left, you'll see a post on your right with green arrows.

At this point you have 2 options. You can carry straight on along the sealed road, turning right immediately after the brick cottage, or turn right onto the dirt path at the green arrow post.

At the first fork take the left. Then left again at the next green arrow towards blue conifers and silver birches. You'll see the brick cottage left. As you draw level with it, you'll see the CP rear entrance.

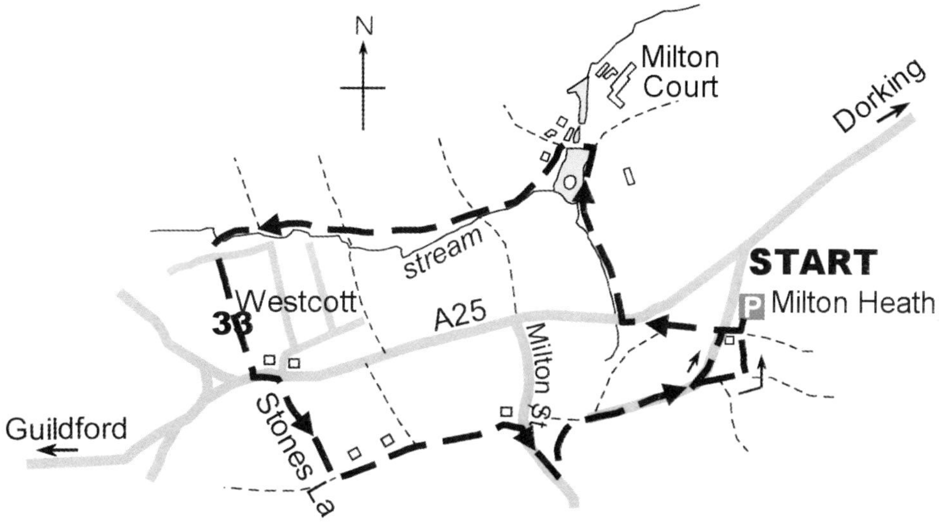

19. BROCKHAM GREEN, PILGRIMS WAY, NORTH DOWNS

Mostly easy, 4½ miles—one long climb

Maps SSA P106 C1 OS SSA p137 B7
Start near the Dukes Head on Brockham Green.

With the pub on your left, walk into the cul-de-sac which leads to The Brockham Pound. (see map). After reading about the pound, turn left on to the public bridleway. After this winding path crosses the Mole River, turn right onto a wide track which climbs gently.

At the top of the incline, with your back to the river, take the car width track, (Mill Hill Lane), toward the North Downs. You'll have houses right and an open field left. Go straight across a sealed back road and continue up Mill Hill Lane. It finally becomes narrow footpath width after the dwellings, with hedgerows on either side, and views to the North Downs.

Keep straight on over the crest of the hill and down to another sealed back road. Cross straight over. The path continues on the other side, with a large pub left, and brings you out at the A25.

Cross the A25 and walk about 5–10 steps right, looking for the stile in the hedge left, leading you into the field. Follow the power lines and rough path across the field to the railway line. (It's rough underfoot.)

Cross the stile and turn right with the railway line running parallel left. At the end of this track turn left under the railway arch. Cross the stile into the pig field. (They're fenced off). Once again it's a bit rough under foot. Cross diagonally right towards an electricity pylon, then just short of the pylon follow the wide track up the middle of the field. At the top end of this field is another stile, bringing you to The Pilgrims Way.

Turn left along the Pilgrims Way, and stay on it for about a mile. You'll pass through Brockham Lime Works. The path keeps right of the derelict buildings.

As you glimpse Brockham, (from whence you came) you'll enter a Yew grove. At the end of this grove you'll come to some wide wooden gates (new). There's a WW2 bunker left. Turn right up hill. This is a long and fairly steep up. Take your time. You will be rewarded.

When you see some obvious well made steps left, with the NDW acorn sign accompanying it, leave the path and take the steps.

These steps bring you on to a U bend in a generous path. Walk left downhill. The views are spectacular to Leith Hill, Dorking and beyond The descent easy. You'll pass Dukes Plantation, where 12,00 Yew trees are planted.

As you progress down hill on to National Trust land, you lose the views for a while, but the path is green and leafy with plenty to see in the hedgerows. A few steps before this wide path reaches a wide metal gate, you'll see a narrow path left. Follow this down between 2 fence lines. It brings you on to a narrow sealed lane. Walk downhill, past Alexander Motors farm left and some houses right.

When the lane curves left, don't follow it, continue straight on down hill to the bridge and cross the river. This brings you out beside Dorking Garden Centre, and to the busy A25.

Cross straight over to the entrance of the golf club on the other side. Turn left at the Stop Look Right sign. (This is barely a hill).

At the U bend where you'll see the club house to the right, keep straight on, to the obvious wide footpath ahead.

You're now on the Old Coach Road which runs between the golf course and Brockham Green. It's flat but pretty with plenty to see.

Towards the end of this road you'll pass Riverdale house left, covered with wisteria in April. After Elm Grove farm turn left over the brick bridge and after a 100 yds or so and a slight rise, you're back at the Green.

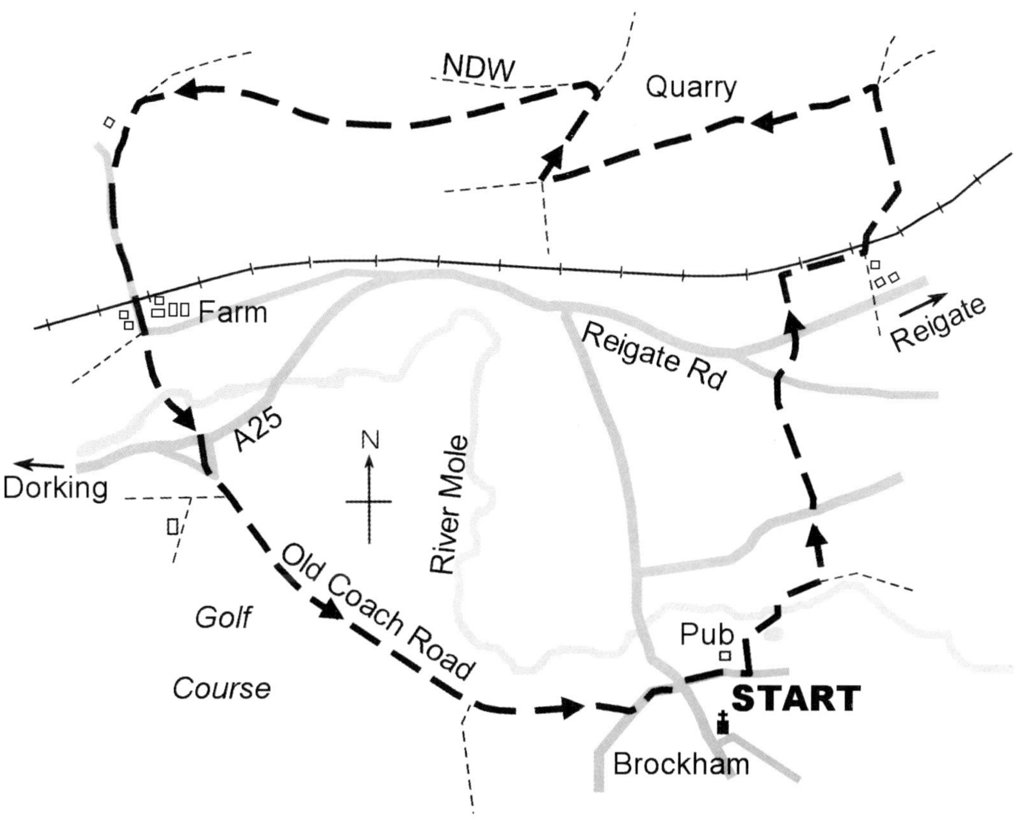

20. SOUTH OF MILTON HEATH

Easy, 4 miles. One hill

Maps SSA P105 E2 OS SSA p135 E6
Start at Milton Heath CP

From Dorking drive west on A25. Just out of Dorking follow sign on left, 'Bury Hill Fisheries'. Once you've turned left off the A25, ignore CP immediately right by A25 and drive 100 yards or so to the large bumpy parking area (signed CAR PARK) first left.

Leave the car park walking between the 2 stout round wooden posts just right of the information board. Go straight across the road and follow the lime green arrows up hill. (The track winds right until reaching the 3rd green arrow.) Cross the dissecting path from this post to another post with orange arrows, and turn right.

Follow the next orange arrow up hill (do not talk until you reach the top!) to the temple. It's worth the climb for the fine views, north to Denbies and Ranmore, and south to Leith Hill, and a little further along, unusual views down over Dorking, and along the NDW to Brockham quarries.

From the temple walk along the wide ridge path in the direction of Dorking, soon an easy descent.

At the T junction, by a wooden seat, turn left down into the grassy Nower and Milton Heath Park. Head for the gate in the picket fence just right of another SCC information board.

This brings you to Coldharbour Lane. Cross and turn right, walking along the footpath to the junction Of Knoll Road. Cross and walk up Ridgeway Road. Keep to the right side and just before it bends left, leave the road, following the wooden footpath sign to the right.

This path runs for a short distance between 2 fences, and soon brings you in to Coldharbour Lane allotments, then out through a kissing gate, passing under a huge oak. You'll see a few houses left.. Keep straight on, coming to open fields, with power lines left and ahead, and you'll hear traffic to left and ahead.

On reaching the lowest point in the field you'll pass through a band of trees from one field to the next. Turn left with the trees left and a church in view ahead.

Follow the path a hundred yards or so, with a hedge left now and a fence right. You're very close to the A24. Once you see it your path runs between conifers right and a wire fence left. This bit of path (rough at first) quickly brings you to farm buildings.

Keep these buildings right, and a house left, and follow wooden finger post with yellow arrow (on your left) over a stile and into field.

At time of writing the path through the middle of the field runs between 2 electric fences. At the end of the field, there's another stile and a well marked wide track. (no electric fence now). Yet another stile at the end of this field, but at present no fence attached!

Keep on more or less straight ahead, on this wide track, now with trees and a stream right. At the end of the field, you'll reach a wide metal gate and stile (with yellow arrow). Cross and walk along right boundary. Keep an eye out for a stile in this right boundary fence. When you reach it, cross and walk up the obvious track in the middle of the field, towards the house on the near horizon.

This brings you to yet another stile and the road (Cold harbour Lane). Cross with care as there's a blind bend right. Turn left along the footpath, past two cottages and a bungalow. Then turn right, after the post box.(sign says Chadhurst Farm). Follow the farm track, to this beautiful building, with views on all sides.

At the pond on your left, there's a wooden finger post with two arrows. Take the right path, not turning right immediately after the house, but walking towards the farm buildings, then turning right downhill along a grassy lane (see map). Here you have a view of Ranmore church spire, which can be seen from a remarkable number of places.

Until you reach the open field at the end of this lane you have hedgerows on either side. Once you cross into the field, keep the ditch close right. At the far end of this field, you'll reach a second wide metal gate in the left corner. From here the path runs between trees and a hedgerow.

Keep with this path, past the fishing ponds until the path runs in to a road, (Milton Street). Keep straight on along this road and turn right at the first footpath you come to (only a short distance once you're on the road.)

This path climbs gently, passing a sandstone cottage on your right. Veer right after this cottage and pass through the wide white gate.

This brings you on to a narrow sealed road. Turn left following this road downhill. As the road curves left, you'll see a post on your right with green arrows.

Carry straight on along the sealed road, turning right immediately after the brick cottage. A hundred yards or so you'll be at the rear entrance of the car park.

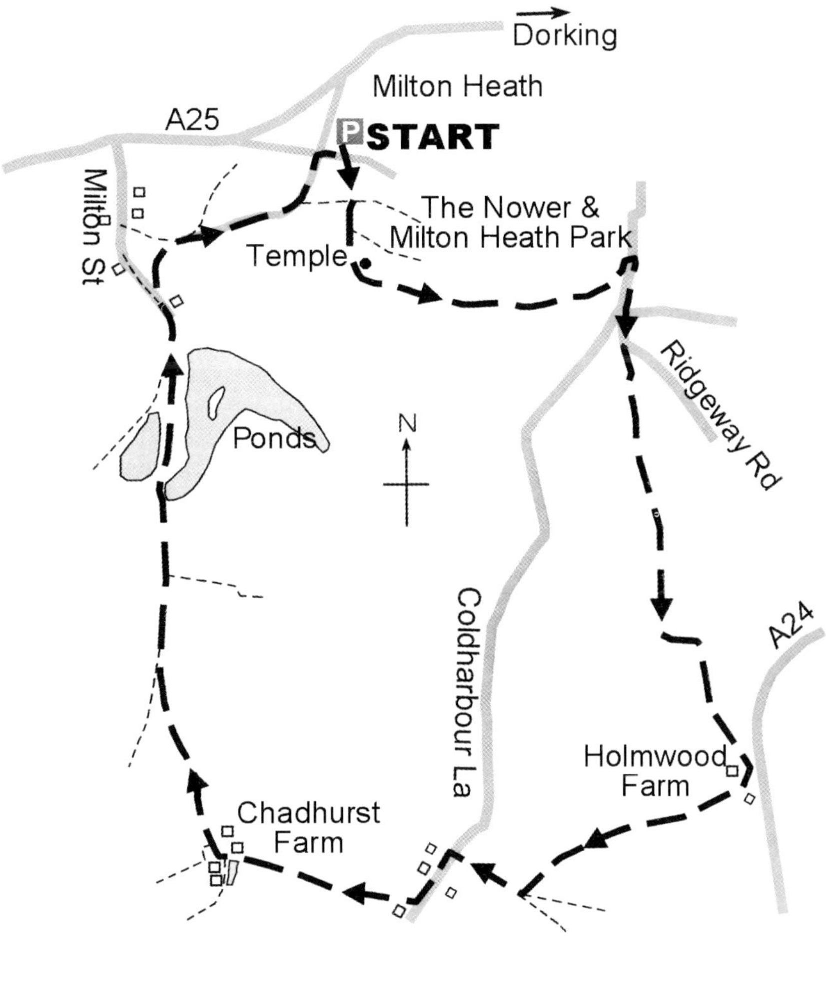

21. LLAMAS DALLY & WILD FOWL RALLY— EFFINGHAM PONDS

Easy, flat, 4 miles.

Full of interest, suited for any time of year.

Wellies or boots when wet.

Maps SSA P85 F1 OS SSA p93 F2
Start near the junction of Sole Farm Road and Little Bookham Street. If driving park in Soul Farm Road and walk back. There is a bus stop outside the PO.

Cross Little Bookham Street from Soul Farm Road and you'll see a wooden footpath sign pointing up a wide entrance road. (As you stand on the PO side of the rd this opening is 2 houses to the left of the post Office.

Walk up this short entrance road and turn right, passing a brick garage left, which brings you promptly to a low stile. Once over the stile the path runs between houses to a street

Keep straight on (don't turn right along this road) watching for a tall metal footpath sign left. This takes you across a small stream (dry in summer), through a narrow band of woods, then between a narrow stile into a field, a large house right.

Keep on with the hedge/ boundary immediately right. At the far end of the field pass through another stile into the woods. Ignore the arrow right and keep straight on. At a T junction turn left along a wider track, then right (after 50 yards or so) onto a pebble farm track.

Follow this pebble track as it curves right until you reach the wide gate at its end. There's a stile immediately left of this gate. Pass through it and keep straight on with the wire fence right. This soon brings you to another stile, and shortly a third.

Once through this third stile walk diagonally right across the field to the stile and wide gate opposite. Follow the worn path keeping the pond right. It's only fifty yards or so to another stile and wide gate. Keep on just about straight ahead.

You'll soon spot the next stile ahead in the fence line, and you'll hear the cacophony (perhaps music to some) of wild fowl right and glimpse the pond just right of the stile.

Turn right and follow the fence line most of the way to the next stile at the end of the field. You'll have a clear view of the pond. And yes, another stile.

Once through the stile, walk over a plank bridge. Turn left for 3 or 4 paces, then right with a pond now on each side of you. At the wide wooden plank bridge you'll have your best and closest view of the wild fowl.

When you're ready move on to the next stile and into the field. Walk past the large fenced tree to the hedge and turn right with the hedge left. Walk along this boundary until you reach a wide gate with a metal ladder stile.

Turn left here and walk up this road (Lower Farm Road) until you reach the Common Road at the other end. Turn right along the footpath for 50 yards. Cross the road and walk up the driveway just right of the post box. You'll see 3 houses on front of you. Keep to the right edge of this drive and turn right onto the grass as soon as there's enough grass to walk on, following this right edge where mown grass meets untamed area.

Head for a dark wooden building and pass through a narrow gate to it's right, (there's a yellow arrow on right), and along the drive which takes you out to a wide farm track.

Turn left along this farm track and walk along it until you reach a pond on your left. At the end of the pond you'll come to a footpath right. Turn right here following another yellow arrow. There's a brick cottage immediately right and you're walking beside the wire boundary fence.

Follow this path through a narrow band of woods, into a field. Keep on the narrow well worn path as it runs along the right edge of the field. When you reach a point where there's a vehicular track running right into the next field, turn right into this field and walk across to the boundary where field meets wood. Swing right along this boundary with the field on your right now and woods beside you left.

You'll see and hear traffic on the common road to your far right. Follow the boundary of woods and field until you see some bungalows ahead. Now swing diagonally right across the field aiming for the woods to the right of the bungalows. Once again walk along the edge of the woods and field to the road.

Go straight across and walk up the private road entrance a few yards, (permissive footpath and bridleway). After a few steps you'll reach a footpath to your right branching away from the road. Take this path through the woods.

It will lead you to a small clearing and two wide metal gates. Cross the stile left of the second gate and walk along the wide grassy path between two fences. At the end of this fenced in section, cross the stile and walk along the obvious path through the middle of the field. There's a ditch right now.

It's very pleasant walking with plenty of wide open spaces, variety and interest. Cross the high stile at the end of the field and you'll find yourself passing under a railway line to another high stile, then another stretch of wide path between 2 wire fences. If you pause at the gate post on your left you can learn about the Camelid family. (If the info's still there)

At the end of this stretch between fences, cross the stile (a yellow arrow on one side of it). The path runs across a wooden footbridge into the woods, with a ditch left and an old wire fence right.

When the path emerges at a T junction, turn right on to the wide dirt path passing a N T sign left which says Bank's Common. Easy walking here with the woods right and a field left. At the end of the field keep straight on, as the path widens to a farm track.

Keep straight on over a stream, past 3 cottages, and silver birches. As the farm track turns a corner to the right, stay with it passing another NT sign left saying Bookham Common, then cross a cattle grid.

The rest of the walk continues in this direction. The farm track leads into a sealed road. When this road curves sharp left, leave it, continuing straight ahead into Maddox Lane, Bookham Grange Hotel left. A brick bridge takes you over the railway line.

At the end of Maddox Lane, cross Maddox Park (sealed road) and walk along the narrow boundary footpath, straight across another sealed road, over a wooden plank bridge and follow your nose back to Little Bookham Street.

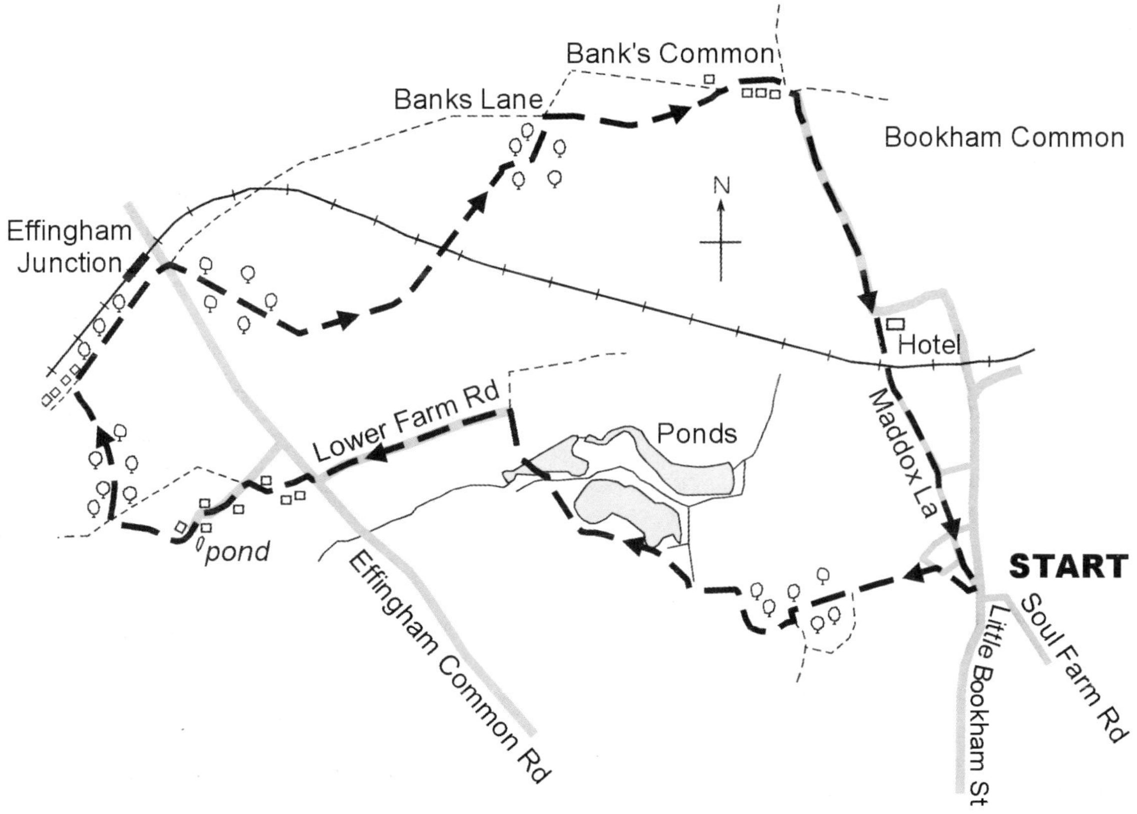

22. WOTTON, FRIDAY STREET & THE TILLINGBOURNE

Undulating, $4^2/_3$ miles

Maps SSA P104 C3 OS SSA p 134 F4
Start at the back of Wotton Hatch Hotel, on the A25 between Dorking and Gomshall. There's a bus stop right outside, and a large carpark at the back. The owners are happy for walkers to park here but would appreciate it if you'd let them know you're there.

Walk away from the Pub and cross the wooden stile into the green field. passing the community hall right. Head slightly diagonally right to the far end of the field. You'll see a stile about 50 yards before the end of the field, in the fence on your right. Cross and turn left still moving in more or less the same direction, and walk along the sealed road, which curves right and gently downhill.

When the holly hedge left ends there's a stile, and a wooden finger post footpath sign. Bear in mind that any wet wood may be slippery. Cross it and walk down the fence line to the next stile and across a small brook. Once across the brook, there's a fence right.

At a T junction, turn right then follow the path as it veers left., passing a wide metal gate right and a sign inside the property saying 'Wotton Estate, Private'.

The path now runs beside 2 wire fences with lovely views right down to a chain of weirs. The walk's very easy from here. You're going to continue in this direction for some time now, more or less in a straight line.

You'll finally be confronted with a wide wooden gate, with a yellow arrow on the post to the left of it, and a stile. Once over the stile, there's a bridge right, a pleasant spot for reflection before continuing on in the same direction, with the weirs still to your right.

You'll come to a cottage right, then another left which is soon obscured by the trees. A little further on the stream actually crosses the path. A short distance past here is another cottage left, just before you arrive at Friday Street.

Keep on in the same direction with the Friday Street pond on your left. This road leads to the pub and a few cottages. The last cottage, on your right is called Lane End.

Now the way becomes a muddy track through woodlands, leading after 10–20 minutes to more cottages and a sealed road.

Turn left on to this sealed road and stay with it as it curves left, then sharply left as you pass Spring Cottage and walk up hill.

As the road's about to swing right, leave it, following the wooden footpath sign left down a driveway to two cottages, Beechwood House and Lemon's Croft.

Take the path that runs uphill between the two houses, right past the windows of the house on your right. Keep on until you reach what looks like a low metal fence ahead of you. At the left end of this metal fence is a stile of sorts to pass through. Go on up the hill.

At the top of the hill, you come out at a field and the path immediately veers left into another field. Follow the right hedge line and continue in a straight line until you come to a wide gate and a narrow road. This grassy level stretch is ideal for a picnic on a sunny day.

Cross the road to the wooden footpath sign and follow the arrow. You're now on the homeward stretch, and a gentle descent. There are short wooden finger posts at regular intervals along this stretch through the bracken.

Keep an eye out for the finger posts with the yellow arrows. You'll eventually be heading fairly steeply down hill in places and still steadily diagonally right. There are several possible paths, but if you keep an eye on the map, you'll find they all lead to Rome.

Don't descend too soon. When you do, you'll see a house and a couple of chimneys through the trees. Keep above that house. You'll slowly move closer to the houses, descending all the time. Don't walk into someone's back garden. The path winds along the back of 2 or 3 homes.

A few paces after you reach a wooden power pole, turn right between two houses down a well trodden narrow track. This runs down to a sealed road. Swing left along this road, walking past Leith Cottage on left.

Walk on down the road until you reach the Triple Bar Riding Centre left, and just as you're almost past the riding centre, turn right along a dirt track that says Public Footpath. This path follows the Tillingbourne, for most of the homebound journey. You'll pass a man made water fall right, a little way along this track.(It can be very mucky on this section if there's been rain.)

The track finally rises to a point where it levels out and you have a view up to the NDW, an open field right. Stay with this track until it runs into a sealed road.

As soon as you've passed between the two brick gate posts, take a couple of steps right, then walk left along the fence line. There's a field right, with some disused low lying farm buildings and the road left, hidden by the trees.. You're still looking up to the NDW.

As soon as there's an opening big enough to pass through on your left, turn along it and onto the road. This brings you out by Sheep-house Green. Turn into the Green, and walk along the footpath on the right side, which soon veers right, departing from the road.

Keep an eye on the map, and keep heading slightly right when there's the option, until you reach a short path that runs through a small patch of wood. These woods end at a stile which brings you back into the field in which you started. There's a brick house right with a dovecote. Turn right at the corner and you're back.

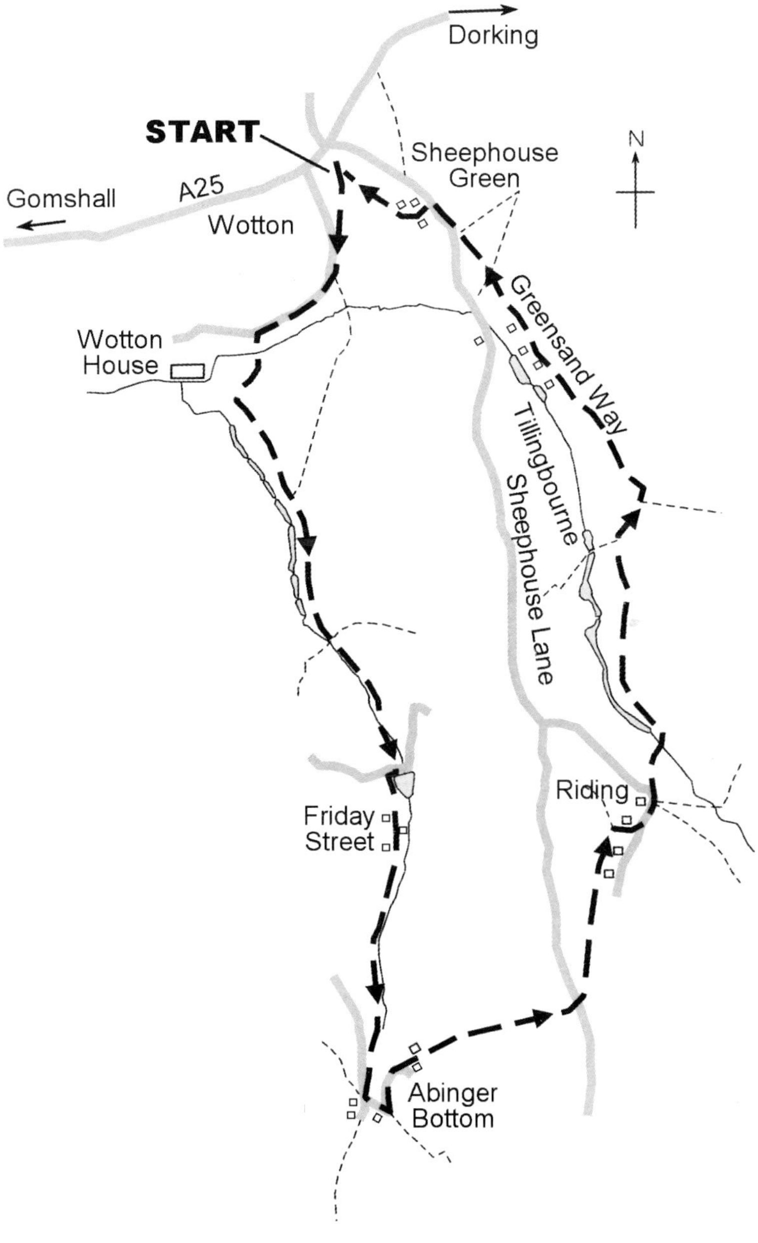

23. A CIRCULAR WALK FROM EFFINGHAM

Undulating, 5 miles. Bluebells in May

Maps SSA P85 F3 OS SSA p113 F5
Start Top of Woodlands Road, where the sealed road ends (parking at sides of road). Walk or drive up Woodlands Road (off A246).

Walk straight on up a wide dirt track. After 100 yds or so you'll come to a junction, with a wooden footpath sign by a path immediately right. There's another path passing through wooden kissing gates, a little beyond this first, which also swings right.

Take the immediate path right, which runs in a straight line with a barb wire fence left and woods on the right. As the woods end, you'll come to an open field right and now a fence on either side of you. At the end of the wooden fence you'll come to a stile. Cross into the field and continue in the direction you've been walking, towards the far corner of the field.(see map)

In this corner there's a wide wooden gate with a stile at one side. (There's another wooden gate a little to the left of this with an obvious NT sign by it.) Cross the stile and turn right along the path. Follow this path until you reach High Barn Road. Just before you reach the road you'll pass a large building left, then High Barn Farm right.

Cross the road, take a few steps right then left, following the fingerpost arrow, onto a nice wide grassy path heading in the same direction. There's now an open field right, scrub left. and a wire fence either side, with views right towards Windsor Castle. This is easy under foot, not muddy at time of writing (late Nov).

Keep on in this direction until you come to another sealed road (Beech Avenue). Cross the road. The path continues on the other side. There's another wooden footpath sign by the sign that says Warren Field. Walk along the wide track, with a conifer hedge right. When this ends you'll come to 2 wooden posts. Walk between these two posts onto a golf course. Watch out for flying missiles! Study the map carefully at this point.

Walk straight across towards a silver birch. There's a golf tee to your left so keep an eye in that direction for golfers. As you reach the silver birch which is slightly right of a large clump of trees, you'll see a short wooden post with a yellow arrow, just to the left of the Silver Birch, saying public footpath. Follow in the direction of the arrow.

Walk on slightly to the left towards a drinking fountain at the side of a wide golf path. There's a green right, and before you reach the fountain there is another post with 2 yellow arrows. Swinging south west-ish, walk along the edge of the clump until you reach a corner and see a sand bunker in front of you.

Looking across the bunker, facing the tree line on the far side of the fairway there's another short wooden post with a yellow arrow on it, This may be difficult to spot amongst the Hawthorn, depending on the time of year. There's a group of conifers ahead to your right and a black and white stripey pole left. The wooden finger post lies between these two land marks. If you can't see it, cross in that direction and look for it.

Once you reach the finger post, the path is obvious. Stay on this path as it meanders through the woods. Shortly after an easy descent, and some level walking, (which will be muddy after rain), you'll see buildings right beyond a chunky split rail fence.

At this junction, turn left along a level farm track, running about due south. When you reach two houses left, walk past and at the boundary fence of the second, turn left (east), following a green metal sign. You're walking between 2 fences now. You'll come to a wooden stile. Cross and walk on more or less straight ahead. This is the bluebell patch.

This path wends through the woods and brings you to another stile and open fields. Cross and walk on straight ahead following the fence line left. Across to your right you can see several larger buildings, one of which used to be The Old Cart Lodge.

At the end of the field cross another stile and turn right along the farm track. Pass through the wide green metal gate, and just beyond this you'll see a footpath sign pointing left. (There's a stile into the field just before you reach the sign.)

Cross into the field and walk along the fence line, (right) almost to the end of the field. You'll come to another green metal footpath sign pointing right. As you're facing this stile, if you look carefully, you'll see another footpath sign ahead pointing left. Turn left when you reach it.

Cross the stile and follow the path keeping fairly close to the fence line left. It's a bit rough under foot here. You'll come to a fence and you'll see once again a post and yellow arrow, and a stile. Cross and walk on. You'll see a sealed road ahead at the bottom of a slight descent. As you reach the road veer right a little and cross to the next footpath sign on the other side of the road. Now you've a short climb. At the top cross the stile and walk into a field.

The footpath continues with the fence left and fields and houses either side. As you draw near to the next stile you're going to cross, you'll see a group of large buildings to your left, which is St Teresa's Convent. Once you cross this stile you're walking along a trackway, for a 20–30 yards. Your path crosses a sealed farm track and after crossing this sealed lane you've got a short but steady descent, with a white house right. When you reach the bottom of the hill, go on straight ahead up the other side between two wire fences and trees.

You'll come to another sealed road (Stonyrock Road) and there's a house left, and a sign on the other side of the road saying no horses. Continue down this wide track until you reach a junction. Turn left down Hogden Lane and walk along it for a mile or so. Mind your ankles. It's a bit rough.

When you reach a point where an obvious wide muddy bridleway exits right, you'll see a short wooden post with a red and blue arrow. Another path runs sharp right of this bridleway, diagonally right up a grassy field.

Walk on a few more yards until you reach another short wooden post with red and blue arrows.

Turn left, following the blue arrow uphill, along a fence line left. Keep on to the top of the hill until you come to a junction.

You'll see a wooden split rail fence right with a kissing gate. Pass through this gate (right).

Follow this path as it continually curves left until you come to another almost identical wooden gate and fence. You're almost back to the start point. You'll see houses, and Woodland Road through the trees.

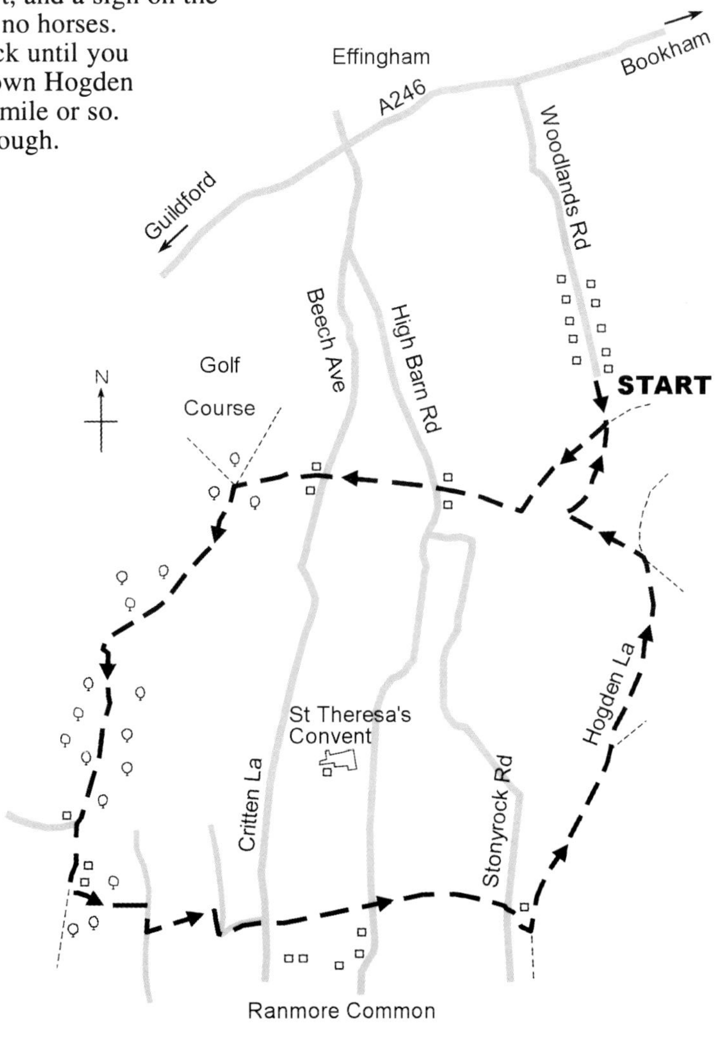

24. EPSOM DOWNS

Easy, undulating, $4\frac{1}{2}$ miles

Maps SSA page 71 F2 OS SSA p77 A1
Start at CP next to Epsom Race Course at Tattenham Corner.

With your back to the road, walk onto the road which crosses into the race course. Walk along the wide track leading to the horizon, with the grandstand not far to your right. There are sky larks, and this first breezy stretch is ideal for flying kites.

It's a barely noticeable incline, with trees on the near horizon in front of you. You'll see a lot of railing ahead of you as you draw close to the trees. Walk on, crossing the race course. (There's a big sign on your left 'Please keep Off the Course'.)

Keep straight on, along the gravel track. You can see the spire of Headley church, slightly left of straight ahead. When you reach a track which dissects yours diagonally from right to left, swing left on to this new track, more in the direction of Headley spire.

On the brow of a hill, you'll reach a sign that says 'Caution Dead Slow'. Race horses crossing ahead. (Give them a wide berth.) Keep straight on, crossing the ride. You can see the spire more clearly now, slightly right of your path.

From here your track heads downhill (a comfortable slope) towards farmland. At the bottom of the hill cross a practise track again, keeping a watchful eye.

Turn left along a vehicle track that runs just below and parallel with the practise tracks. Walk along this track about 100 yards or so. When you reach a point where the track you're on swings to the left, you'll see a white arrow left that says permissive horse ride. (There's also a yellow arrow right on a wooden post saying Public Footpath.)

Turn right on to the horse ride track and walk up hill through a patch of light woodland. When you reach a point with a track coming in from your left, and a wooden finger post with blue arrows pointing in both directions, swing right. (There's a rather dilapidated bylaws board on your left.)

As you reach another wooden finger post, with a blue and yellow arrow, you'll glimpse houses through the trees. Keep straight on here. Ignore the track left and keep the houses left and a wide open field right. The path starts to ascend now, with gardens to admire. It's easy walking just following the boundary.

At the far end of this stretch, the path emerges at some houses and you'll see another footpath sign ahead of you. Keep on more or less straight ahead and turn right as you reach the wooden finger post that says public bridleway (and has a blue arrow). You're still walking along the edge of the houses along a short stretch of partly sealed rather rough road. with fields right,

At a corner, straight ahead of you you'll see a sign saying Derry. Just left of this you'll see a metal PF post/sign. Follow the obvious path uphill between Derry and White cottage.

At the top of the rise, ahead of you, you'll see a wooden footpath marker with arrows pointing left and right. There's a coal tax post and a white barrier left of the footpath sign. Turn right here. There's a high wooden fence right and a mesh fence and what looks like a school left.

When you reach a stile right, turn right across it. The high wooden fence right soon gives way to a wire fence, with a wooden rail fence left. You'll come to another stile at the end of this stretch.

As soon as you cross the stile you're standing by a metal footpath sign which is pointing straight ahead. Continue in the same direction crossing a gravel vehicle track. This time an easy stile to pass through, rather than over, with fields and a view to the Epsom racetrack right. If you look carefully you can see parts of the track you've already walked.

At the end of this stretch you'll come to a sealed road, Ebbisham Lane. Once again the footpath continues on the other side. There is a metal footpath sign but the sign has slipped to the bottom of the post at time of writing. You're in the country again now. Climb over the stile.

Right there's a double wooden fence. About 20 feet to the left of this fence is a line of small old trees. Keep to the tree line and as you reach the fence ahead of you, you'll find another stile. Cross and turn right down hill.

Carry on down this path (about a mile), wending gently downhill until you're close to the race course again. There are beautiful views all round, with Headley spire now left. The descent becomes a bit steeper and rougher as you near the bottom of the hill with No Home Farm left.

As you draw level with the driveway/ entrance of the farm you'll see another footpath/ bridleway sign with a blue arrow. The path turns left. There's now farmland left and Epsom race course right screened by a narrow band of trees.

Pass an obvious turning right, keeping straight on. About 500 yards further on you'll see a track coming in from your left. Ten or 20 paces on from there follow a path up right between two short stubby posts. This will lead you back to Tattenham Corner.

Keep on, crossing the practise track when you reach it, and heading up between white metal barriers. Once again it's barely a hill—just a gentle incline. You've a narrow band of trees left and at this point in time a barrier right.

When you reach a corner where the gravel road swings left, with a house left, follow the track left, then after another 50 yards or so the track swings right. Stay on this track all the way back to the start.

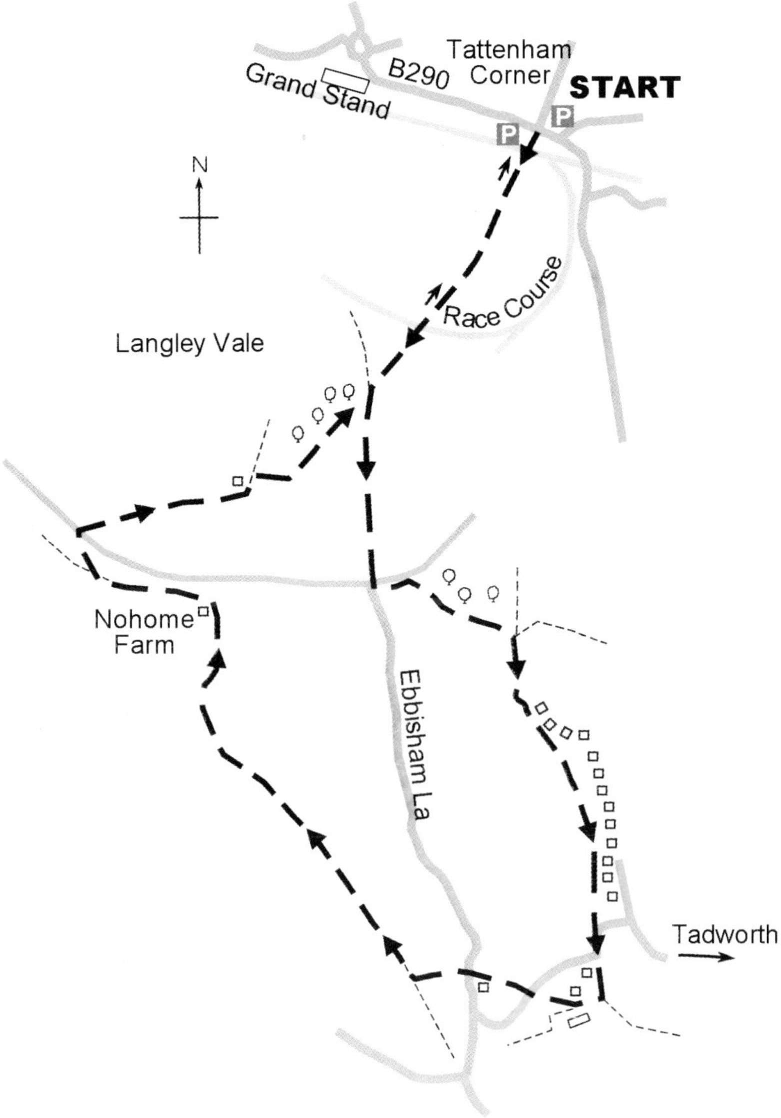

25. WHAT FOLLY! ZIG ZAG TO BOX HILL TO BROCKHAM HILLS

Hilly, 4 miles

Maps SSA Page 87 D3 OS SSA p115 D4
Start at the first car park on left as you walk or drive up the Zig Zag road near Burford Bridge. There is a NT donation box in the car park.

Walk up across the grass to the corner (the first zig.)—cross the road to a low wooden sign that says 'No bicycles.' On your left near the 'No bicycles' sign you'll see a wooden post with a green arrow. Walk up this grassy valley which soon leads into the woods. The grass becomes dirt once you're amongst the trees.

This is a pretty path, a steady climb—not very steep and an easy route up to Box Hill lookout. Stop and rest whenever you need to. Remember to look back from time to time. At regular intervals you'll see short posts with green arrows and numbers. This is part of a nature trail for the NT and their walks are available at the NT shop at the top of Box Hill.

When you come to the road, cross and continue in the same direction. The path soon forks. Take the left fork. You cease to follow the arrow posts from here. Duck under a fallen tree and you're almost at the top of Box Hill. This path swings around to the left a little and brings you out at a clearly defined, light coloured, wide gravel track. Remember this track for later.

Turn right along this track until you come into a clearing, and until the path is about to turn a definite corner to the right. At this point, walk straight on across the grass towards the view which you're already having a glimpse of. You'll see a car park a short distance left and another right. (You're half way between the two.) As you approach the road ahead you'll start to have a view of Dorking,

Cross the road passing close to a sturdy wooden bench left, an ideal spot to sit and admire the view. You can't miss the viewpoint, a memorial to Leopold Salomons who donated this land to the National Trust. Panoramic views from here. If you look slightly left of the viewpoint you'll see a tower and may wonder about it. It's an oilrig.

Once you've taken in the view, walk down the steps right of the memorial on to the wide gravel path. Keep on downhill in to a grove of trees. As you approach a clear area, there's an easily missed path left leading downhill. Take a sharp hairpin turn left here.

More magnificent views on your descent. You'll see further than when you were at the top. Keep following this path until it runs out. It gets steeper but never horribly steep. There's May blossom all around you on this stretch (in May!). When you reach a stile and a wide metal gate in a dark corner of the field under Yew trees, cross the stile and keep on down hill more or less in the direction you've been heading.

You'll see a wide path coming in on your left and your track runs into it. Keep on this rather rutted track down to a sealed lane. Turn left up hill at this junction. After 20–30 yards, you'll reach another junction. You'll see ahead of you 'The Retreat', and just right of this driveway a narrow path with a field right. Walk up this narrow path—about 100 yards or so. If it's summer or late spring there will be nettles so a stick could be handy.

Pause at the top corner of the field for views to Brockham and Betchworth before turning right up the wide easy track. This is uphill walking at it's easiest. You'll hardly know you're climbing. Continue up this pleasing track for a little over a mile.

When you reach a hairpin corner of this path, turn sharp left with it. You're now on the NDW (acorn is symbol). Behind you it runs east down some steps. Keep on along this even gentler incline.

Continue in this direction for ½ mile or so. When you reach a wide white wooden gate that says 'Private', turn left down steep and uneven steps, (which is why the wooden handrail has such smooth edges.) You can see the church at Brockham Green. The path swings right again at the foot of the steps.

As you reach the top of the hill, you'll come to 3 steps and a short post on your left with the acorn sign. There's a path running left to right in front of you. Up to the right is Box Hill Tavern. Cross the path and go up the 4 steps on the other side. The path brings you to 5 more steps then 4 up. There's a yellow arrow pointing left saying public footpath NDW.

Follow this path which runs close to and parallel with the road. Ignore the first track up to your right. Take the second track right which leads to the road. Turn left and you'll see where a path continues on the other side of the road. This takes you through light woodland. You're still roughly parallel with the road.

When you reach a junction after about 60 or 70 yards you'll see a short post with a blue arrow right. Take the path left. This soon crosses a sealed driveway and you can see a house at the far end. Keep straight on, still about parallel with the road.

The path comes quite close to the road and to the car park you saw earlier. Keep on this wide track as it swings away from the road. Ahead of you slightly left you'll see the other car park.

When you reach the wide light gravel path you walked along earlier, turn right and walk all the way down to the folly.(less than a mile) It's a well worn wide path swinging slowly left. It's a shady walk until you're nearly at the end when you come into a clearing.

On your left you'll see West Humble. Keep straight on along this grassy stretch. The path swings slightly right, and you're at the folly and a welcome wooden bench. You'll look down to Juniper Hall, across to Norbury House, and Mickleham Downs.

Retrace about 20 steps and swing right onto the grass downhill to the narrow wooden gate in the fence line. (There's a wire fence about 30 yards to your right). The grassy path gets quite steep as it gets close to the gate. It's easier on your knees if you zig zag slightly. Take care on the little patch of scree just before the gate. It is slippery. Cross the road and turn left about 20 paces go through the gate on the other side.

After a few more steps down there's some more very slippery gravel. Move left on to the grass as soon as you can then head straight down hill, ignoring the first vague track that swings left. Take the next one that is slightly better defined (about half way down the hill side) and follow it left downhill as it runs parallel with the road on your right.

Mind you don't turn an ankle here. The path is narrow, uneven and slopes. Keep your eye on the path and stop when you want to admire the scenery. It soon becomes a well worn dirt track and is easier and more level. At the corner, you'll know where you are. Turn right, cross the road and walk back to the CP.

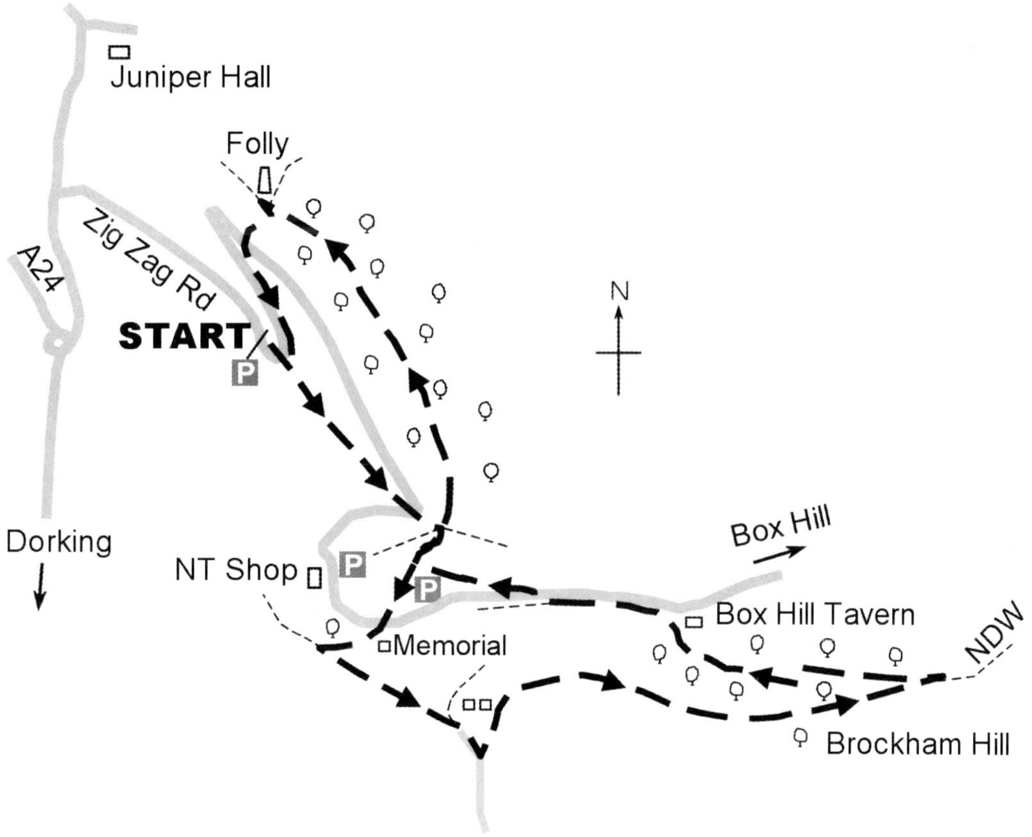

26. SOUTH HOLMWOOD

Hills, 4 miles. Best when dry. Recommended in reverse

Maps SS A Page 125 D1 OS SSA p157 C6
Start just north of the church in Betchets Green Road, South Holmwood. Coming from Dorking on the A24, turn right at South Holmwood sign, just after a BP service station on your right.

Walk down Betchet Green Road to the river/ pond. Once the metal railings by the pond left run out, there's a P F sign left. Pass through the black wrought iron gate, closing it behind you. It feels as though you are walking into someone's garden, but you're not. It is a public footpath.

Walk between two laurel hedges, to another short black painted metal gate at the other end. This brings you out beside a split rail fence left and to a stile. Cross the stile, turn left and follow the path, with another split rail fence right now. There's a stream somewhere near left. Cross a stile into the next field, (full of buttercups in spring).

Keep on with the stream and trees close left and a line of power poles running across the field right. At the corner of the field, you'll come to another stile. Cross and follow the path in the same direction through another field. This will lead you to a shaded stile. Cross and walk along the tunnel of holly. This brings you out at a sealed driveway.

Turn right, turning your back on the noisy road. You'll pass a cottage left. Walk up this sealed lane—a very gentle incline—with azaleas and rhododendrons in a garden left. You'll come to some beautiful buildings. Keep on up hill passing through black metal gates, with a wooden farm building on your left.

The sealed surface ends at the metal gates and is replaced by a wide dirt farm track swinging right. The lane is leafy, with trees either side and occasional speed bumps. Walk on between two solid gate posts. When the road forks at a brick house with lots of chimney pots right, take the left fork.

This brings you to a sealed road. Turn left and follow it a short distance to East Lodge, at the entrance to a private road. Just before it is a path left. This leads you to a stile and into the corner of a green grassy field. Walk up the right side of the field. There's a line of trees right and a worn path across the grass.

As this field ends in the top right corner, you'll come to the remains of a fence and stile (at time of writing). Walk on in the same direction following the path that leads to the corner of the next field. (fine views left). This next corner can be rough and muddy if there have been cattle in the field. Cross the stile, just a few steps then another stile into next field, still walking in the same direction.

The large property quite close left is Capel Leyse. When you reach the shady corner of the field, under a huge oak tree, cross another stile. The path now leads you into a wide farm track curving left a little on to a bitumened surface, and passing a wooden barn like building left.

When you reach a Tee junction, cross the road and take the track on the other side, heading south west. Continue along this wide farm track for just over half a mile until it runs into the corner of a sealed track. You'll see a PF sign on your right pointing to a wide greeny blue metal gate. Pass through it and up the narrow leafy path.

This brings you to another stile in a corner, with a tree handy to pull yourself up on to the stile. There's a fence with two strands of barbed wire right. Continue more or less along this fence line. It's a bit rough under foot here. You'll reach a yellow arrow pointing right with three steps on your right . Cross the stile keeping the fence close right until the path veers left.

This brings you to six more steps and an easy stile because it's broken. Once over the stile there's a wooden farm shelter right. Turn left and walk beside the fence line. There may be horses and a donkey in this field.

When you come to a brick wall, turn left and you'll find yourself walking up a path with chicken wire on one side and a stone wall right. This brings you to a sealed road. Turn right up the road passing several houses left.

As you draw level with Rose Cottage left, turn right and follow the footpath sign, down the lane (Moorhurst Lane) with a 'no through road' sign. This becomes a pleasant shady walk. The track passes under power lines. When you come to a second power pole, keep an eye out for a stile left.

You'll see a footpath sign left just beyond the power pole. You'll also have passed a solid wooden stump, the remains of a tree, right. Cross the stile into the corner of the field. Walk straight on up the hill. This is the beginning of a long uphill—easy if you pause often.

Keep to the right border of this field. Views to right give a good excuse to stop and catch your breath. Higher up views are even better.

Part way up the hill you'll come to a border line where there is a line of trees in front of you, but no longer a fence. You'll see a yellow arrow on a wooden post right. You can see the path now veers left a little. As the ground levels out you'll see a wooden stile ahead of you at a boundary corner.

Closer, you'll see a yellow arrow on it. The path follows the fence line, with a single barb wire strand on top of the fence. There's tree cover along this stretch. When the fence runs out continue slightly left of straight ahead. At another stile you'll see Anstiebury Farm buildings on the sky line.

Head right (north west) diagonally up the field to the right of the farm. You'll reach a stile in the fence. Before you climb over, enjoy the 280 degrees views. You can see to Brockham Lime works and far beyond.

From here it's easy. The path winds downhill in a north-easterly direction. Follow the yellow arrows, past houses, into a cool leafy area, (muddy when wet). Lower down you'll reach a stream, and a grassy field beyond the stream. As the path levels out the shade is less dense. You'll reach a grove of oak trees right.

When the path runs into an open field keep to the right fence line.

You'll come to a cream house right, then reach a gate at the corner of the field. Turn left down the sealed lane. Looking back you'll see this is the private road you saw towards the beginning of the walk. Follow this road back to the church, past Betchetts Green Farm.

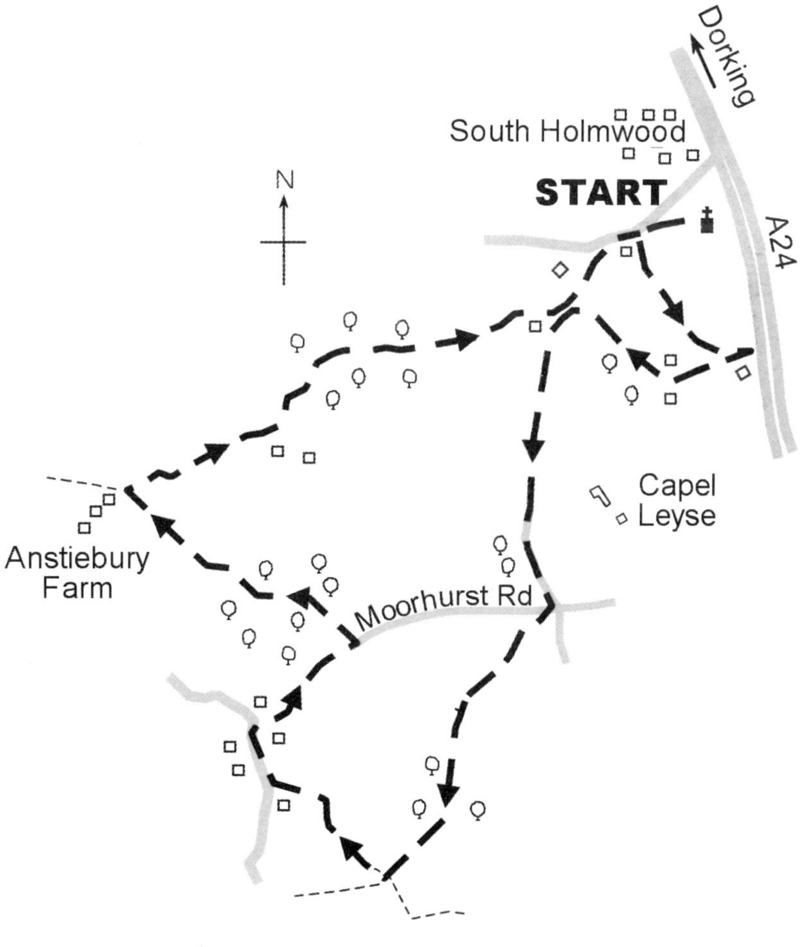

27. FROM BROCKHAM GREEN

Easy, 5+ miles.
Best in dry weather

Maps SSA P106 1 OS SSA p137 B7
Start from the church on Brockham Green.

Turn your back on the church. Cross the road, passing the old village pump, then walk down Old School Lane. This first stretch is part of the Greensand Way. Cross the brick bridge with Brooklands Cottage left and just ahead a Public Footpath sign .

Turn right onto this path which leads you on to The Old Coach Road. Follow this track through the golf course. At a sealed road, you will see the golf course car park left and straight ahead of you a footpath sign pointing to a path right of the car park.

Cross the sealed road on to this path. After about a hundred yards, the path forks, just by the golf house. Keep to the right fork which leads more or less straight on. Reaching a sealed track, you'll see another wooden fingerpost with a yellow arrow on it. Turn right on to this sealed track which leads to Punchbowl Lane.

Turn left into Punchbowl Lane (a fairly busy back road), and walk to the crest of the hill and down the other side a short way to a tall wooden finger post pointing left. This leads in to Park Farm. There's a sign at the entrance, and a cattle grid and kissing gate left of the grid.

You're on the Greensand Way again on a very comfortable sealed drive, with views up to the NDW and Brockham Hills. The path veers left at the bottom of this drive, just after another cattle grid. You'll pass a pond right and beautifully kept farm buildings left. Level with the pond pass through a gateway, (a yellow arrow on right side of gate) on to a dirt track.

Keep the fence close left, passing a stile left. Your path crosses under the railway line into a muddy field at time of writing. Continue straight on towards Brockham. The path is a grassy verge between two fields, (still the Greensand Way). You can see a red brick farmhouse, Pond Tail Farm, ahead of you and a wide section of the North Downs.

As you draw closer to the farm, keep an eye out for a tall wooden finger post left, pointing right. The path does a little wiggle here through the brambles and nettles to take you to the right side of the fence you've been following and to a stile into another field. There are large oaks left and the steeple of Brockham Church ahead.

Continue from field to field until you draw level with Pondtail Farm. At the end of this field there's a stile with 2 yellow arrows on it.(One may be obscured). Cross over and immediately turn left, approaching the farm. Cross the next two stiles then turn right along the farm driveway.

At the sealed road, (School Lane) turn right. Walk past the houses left. Once past them, look out for a lay-by left. There's a gap in the hedgerow. Turn left here across a little bridge, and once across the stile, turn right up onto the footpath, continuing parallel with the road. (The benefits of this vary depending on the season. If it's very wet, it may be advisable to stay on the road.)

Follow the edge of the field until reaching another stile. The path crosses back to the road for a short way. You'll pass by large wooden farm buildings right. When you're more or less level with two brick houses right, just before the road swings right, you'll see a footpath sign pointing left into the field.

Follow the sign keeping the hedge row right. Cross a stile into the next field. Across it you'll have views of Brockham Hills and the NDW and just ahead of you, left, Brockham.

At the end of the field another stile brings you onto a wooden bridge then onto a footpath that runs beside back gardens. Plenty of blackberries here in season.

When you reach a busy road, (Middle Street) cross left to the footpath sign on the other side. Follow the path across the field until you reach another sealed road, (Wheelers Lane). It's very rural and scenic here. Cross and turn right about 50 yards to another footpath sign, just past a large house.

Turn left and follow the gravel track between two houses. Keep on in this direction as the path becomes grassy, hedgerows either side. It changes again to a leafy tunnel. After it swings left, you'll pass allotments and cross a footbridge.

The path finally runs in to Juniper Walk. At the major sealed road, Wheelers Lane, turn right, returning to the church.

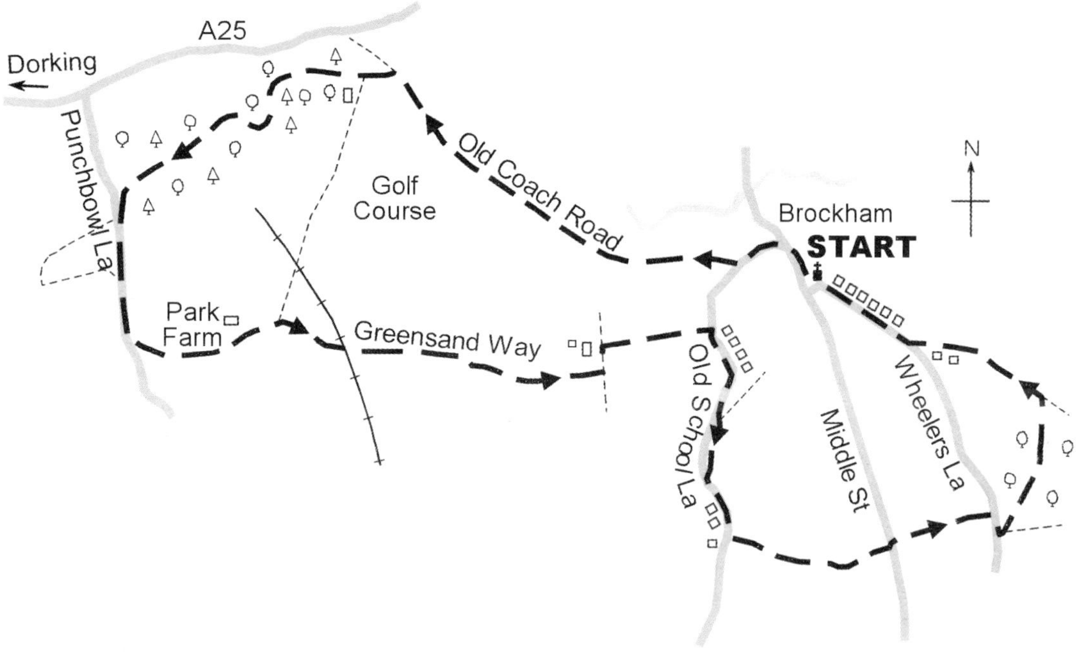

28. WEST, SOUTH AND EAST OF GOMSHALL

Easy, 4½ miles.
Good for winter walking

Maps SSA P103 E3 OS SSA p133 C4
Start at the corner of High View and Queen Street, Gomshall. There's a bus stop here for Tillingbourne Buses, or park along High View.

Face west and cross to Gravel Pits Lane. Walk along the Lane, following the Public Bridleway sign. At a corner where the track swings right, don't. Continue straight on, keeping left of Gravelpits Farmhouse, and passing tennis courts right. The path climbs gently, taking you over a railway bridge, then between two fields, a wire fence either side.

When you reach a junction at the end of the field right, turn right along a well worn track, a fence right, same field right, trees left. (There is a finger post, but arrow faded at time of writing.) Follow path along fence line, then, past several cottages and up to Hook Lane.

Cross then turn right along the lane for 20 or so paces then left, following the FP sign. This drive leads into another field with wide views to the south. Keep to the right fence line. The path runs on, narrow between 2 fences.

At the next junction, Hound House Road, turn left about 30 paces to a 'Public Byway' sign. Next, turn right down the byway passing Parklands Farm and several other cottages left. When you reach the gates at the railway line, ignore them. Swing left, following the red arrow, passing more cottages left.

The track now ascends, between two banks and two fence lines, before descending to Ponds Farm right. Ignore the path right, and look for the path that takes you left across a field and to Hound House Road again.

Turn right along the road to Cotterell Farm, and cottages. Turn left onto the path opposite the farm house. At the top of the rise, the path veers left down to Lawbrook Lane, a hedgerow left, an open field right.

Cross the lane to the kissing gate and Public Bridleway sign, quickly bringing you to Jessies Lane. Turn right, past Oak Farm, (a beautiful farm). Walk on up and around the bend, to a wide gate and stile left. There's a broken footpath sign here at time of writing which is hard to spot.

Once over the stile you're looking at another wide gate. Go through this gate, (not right, up hill). You'll see 2 red brick cottages on the skyline ahead. The level path winds along the bottom of the field, under power lines, bringing you out at a farm.

Turn left along the footpath of Pursers Hollow. Across the road right, is a large wooden building. As you start to ascend you'll come to Broadfield Road on left. It says 'Private Road No bridleway', but it is a public footpath. A few yards up this track, you'll see a stile on your left, just before you reach a wide gate across the track. Cross the stile and follow the short obvious path though the field to another stile.

This second stile brings you back on to Broadfield Road, (and the P F). It's an easy inclining wide dirt track, sheltered between banks and trees. It eventually runs between conifers and cottages up to Pursers Lane. Cross the road and turn right, up the lane.

Just before the crest of the hill turn left into Wonham Way. Look immediately left for a public footpath sign. This points to a diagonal path running between Wonham Way, and a garage marked Glyn. The path runs between back gardens, finally arriving at a Tee junction.

Turn left about 20 yards to a stile right. This leads to a diagonal path across the field, with fine views. When you reach the far fence line, cross the stile and turn right. After the path veers left, you'll come to a junction. Turn right and this bridleway, (muddy when wet) will lead you back to Towerhill then High View.

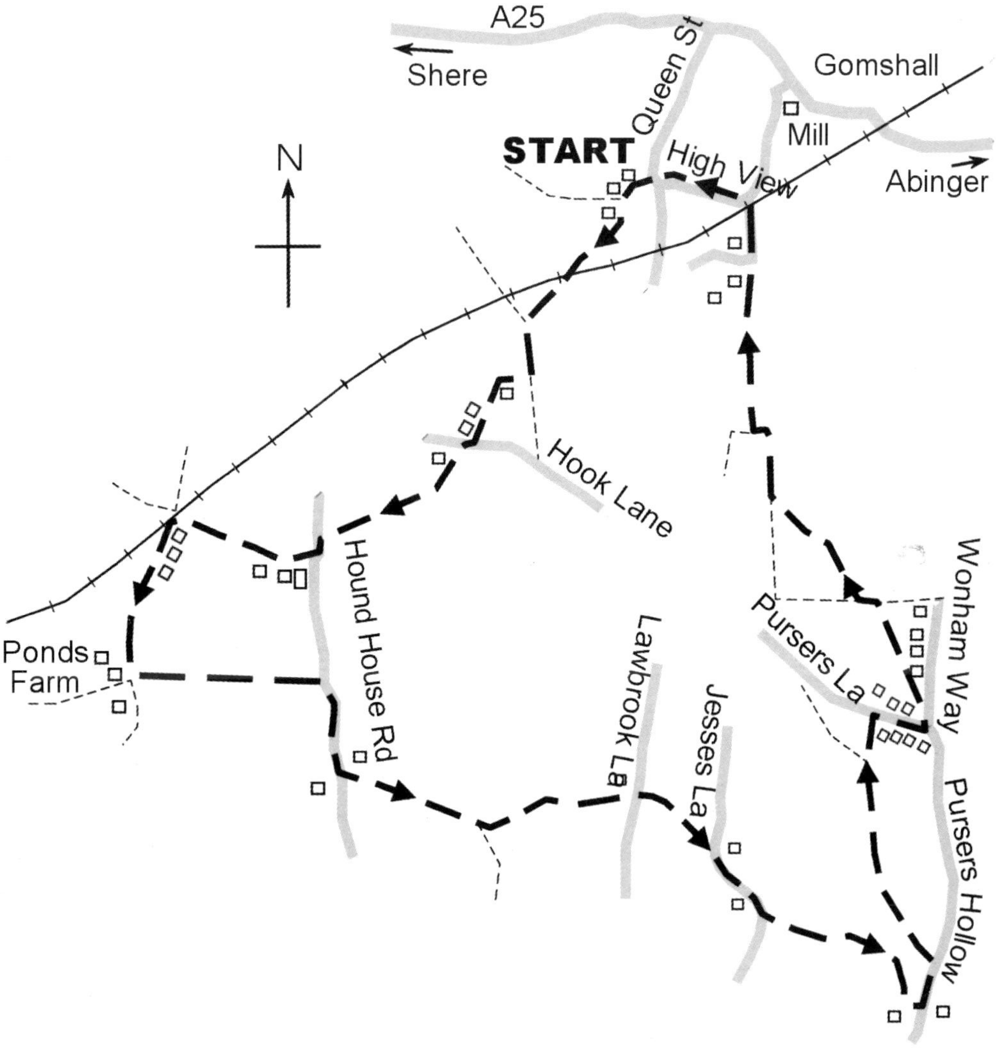

29. REIGATE HEATH

Easy, 4 or 5 miles.
Ideal winter walking

Maps SSA P 89 D5 OS SSA p117 D1
Start from the car park in Flanchford Road, on Reigate Heath just west of Reigate. It's a 5 minute walk from the A25 if you're using public transport.

As you come down Flanchford Road from the A25, walk through the right hand car park to the large oak. There's an obvious path starts under the oak. Follow it away from the road, walking towards the Golf course. Once you have the fairway in view swing left and keep to the oak tree line, heading west. Watch out for golfers and golf balls from behind.

Walking up a slight incline, you'll see ahead of you a well worn path diagonally across the fairway. Once you reach this well worn track, turn right and follow it, still walking slightly uphill. Once across the fairway, and into the trees, you'll find yourself on a sandy path. This will lead you to the windmill and the Clubhouse.

Once you reach a sealed track, a house immediately in front of you, turn left along it, the windmill right. The last building you'll pass will be the Clubhouse.

As the track becomes a single lane, (50 yds in front of the club house) you'll see a short wooden finger post with a yellow arrow, pointing right. Leave the bitumen track, and follow the arrow heading downhill past a seat on your left, through the heather. (At time of writing the path has been redirected as described here).

As you walk down hill you'll come to another fairway, and you'll see a large house the other side of the fairway. A path runs just in front of this house and there's a wooden finger post just left of the house. Cross to this path and turn left, walking up to the corner of Flanchford Road.

You'll see on the other side of the road a tall wooden finger post. Follow that pointer, turning right along Sandy Lane. (Views up to the North Downs right). On reaching Oak house left, take the path immediately after it. There is a finger post but the pointer is broken off at time of writing.

You are now walking up a slight incline between fence lines and trees either side. Follow this wide bridleway up then down the other side to the sealed road, Trumpetshill Road. Turn left onto Trumpetshill Road, passing the Old School House left, then several other houses.

After passing Badgers Holt, you'll come to a driveway right, and a sign saying Public Bridleway. Turn right here on to the drive. After about 20 steps, You'll come to a finger post saying Public Footpath. Follow the arrow, leaving the bridleway/ drive, and walk up a grassy path between 2 fences, past a small house right.

As the fences run out, you'll cross a stile with a yellow arrow. Keep to the right fence line, to a second stile. Cross into a small tree'd section, quickly arriving at a third stile. You're in the corner of a field and it's about 50 yards across it to the fourth stile.

On the other side you'll see several signs. Follow the Public Byways sign left.

Keep on this wide track as it slowly curves left, past a red brick house and a wooden barn right. (Slight incline here. Slightly behind you left, you'll see the North Downs). This leads you to Flanchford road. The path continues on the other side.

You're now on a Public Footpath, an open field right, old pines and a large house immediately left. It's pleasant easy walking for any time of year, especially winter—plenty to see and plenty of variety.

The path leads to a stile which brings you into a field. There may be horses. Walk in the same direction up the field towards the wide wooden gate. (Keep clear of livestock. Don't feed or fondle them.)

Just right of the gate is a stile. Cross, and walk straight ahead along the dirt farm track, towards the brick house and oak tree, There are wooden and wire mesh fences either side of you. At an intersection, keep straight on passing the red brick farm house right.

At the entrance to the farm, veer left along the cement track, to a junction, your back to the farm. At the junction at a public footpath and a bridleway sign, swing right along the bitumen lane. There are stout wooden railings on either side. Walk on up this lane as it climbs to Park Hill.

By the time you reach the crest of the hill and the junction, you'll be well warmed and glad to look back at the view.

Cross the road, go up the steps and if you'd like a longer walk, turn right. For the shorter walk turn left to the Priory Pond. For a third option, if you're feeling energetic and it's a clear, dry winters day, go straight ahead up the hill. It's easy to get your bearings here which ever way you go. The eventual object is to reach the pond.

If you opt for the longer walk, keep on along the track. It's easy walking and good under foot. As you reach the far end of the hill you'll hear then see Park Lane East. The path curves left, another path coming in from the left.

Just as you see the corner of Park Lane East right, you'll see a well defined path ahead of you. Just before you reach it turn left (just after a finger post with a yellow arrow which points up the hill) down hill on a path that runs through the trees. There's a slight gully right.

As you progress the track becomes a well worn path through the grass. You're right on the south edge of Reigate. Before you reach the green playing fields of the park, there's a path left, just inside the tree line. Walk this way, or down on to the grass then left, whichever takes your fancy.

As you see the pond, walk towards it and around it anti clockwise. There are seats, picnic tables, and many open beaks. Continue around, past the popular feeding spot. After crossing a bridge over the out flow, turn right immediately, tall green laurels right.

This leads you to the road, (Park Lane). The path continues on the other side. There is a stream right and allotments right of the stream. This footpath runs in to a farm track. There may be a patch or two of mud but easy to avoid. Follow this track all the way back round to Littleton Lane (Greensand Way).

Turn right down the Lane. You're retracing your footsteps here, just for a short way. At the junction, take the bridleway to Reigate Heath, (the path right). This stretch does get chewed up when wet, but is better than it looks at edges . Once over the crest, you'll pass the Skimmington Castle. As you draw level with a white cottage on your left, you'll see a finger post and a path right

Follow the blue public bridleway sign. You're still on the Greensand Way, with the golf course left. After 50 paces or so, at another short wooden finger post, turn left on to a less well defined track, passing two golf tees right, then moving into the trees. Follow your nose the short distance from here to the car park.

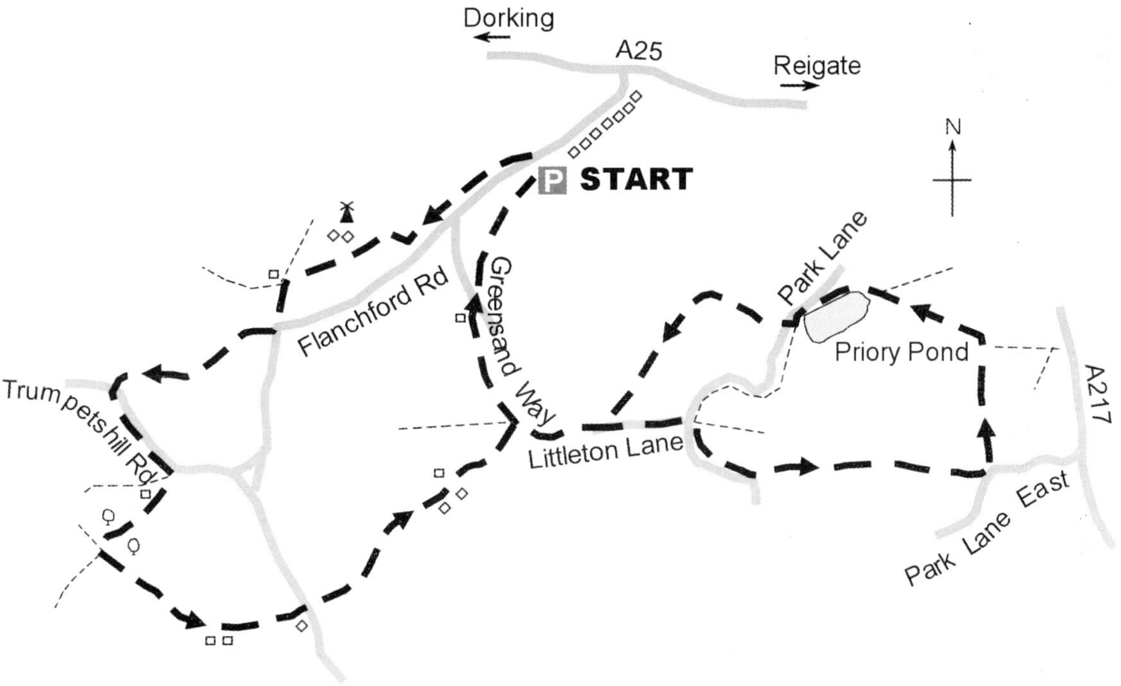

30. ABINGER TO BROOMY DOWNS

Undulating, 4½ miles.
Bluebells in May

Maps SSA P104 B5 OS SSA p155 D8
Park along Green near church at Abinger

Standing in the church CP facing the pub, back to the church, turn left along road a few steps, then right following yellow arrow up drive. Pass The Rectory and school left, following the paving slabs to the kissing gate. Walk on down the path. When it forks take the right path. (Bluebells here in May.) Keep on walking downhill in more or less the same direction until you reach a cream house left. Pass on by this house to Hollow Lane and a bus stop.

Turn left downhill passing a row of cottages left. After the last and largest house, turn left on to a P F, and over the stile on to a wide muddy(in winter) path. Follow this path to Abinger Lane at the other end. Turn right, passing Abinger Mill and a tennis court right. At Raikes Lane, turn right towards the A25.

After about 75 yds turn left over stile into a field, at a wooden finger post. Crossways Farm is nearby right. Walking slightly right of parallel to the stream, look to the fence line towards the far end of the field. You'll see a house on the other side of the A25 and just in front of the house, (in the field) another stile.

Once across this stile, cross A25 and follow the P F sign, with the farmhouse close left. Keep walking, a fence soon left. Pass the walled gardens walking straight on until you reach a wooden stile.

Cross in to the field and follow the faint worn grassy path up to the tree line. Once into the trees you'll reach a distinct path running left to right. Ignore it and continue straight on up the gentle incline past a wooden post with yellow arrow, right in front of an oak.

As you walk through a patch of bracken you'll come to a wide green swathe of path bearing diagonally left. Walk up here a short way to a squat low oak, with another finger post in front of it. Turn right here up towards a wooden seat at the next tree line.

Take note of your surroundings here so you can get your bearings in 20 mins time when you'll emerge on this same track about 50 yds left. There's a blue arrow on the wooden finger post, left of the seat as you face it.

Follow this arrow straight on, on a well defined sandy path. (Don't stray on to the immediate path departing left.) Follow this sandy track up, then down hill, turning sharp left at a wide farm track. (If you get as far as the railway line you've gone too far.) You'll see Hackhurst Farm ahead right. At the next junction, looking down to the farm, turn left up hill on to another farm track.

At the crest of the hill turn left again up farm track. There's a post with a blue arrow on your left after 15 paces or so. You'll soon reach two short wooden finger posts on right, about 10 feet apart. Walk on down to the second and take a hairpin turn to right then downhill to a 5 bar gate. There's a gap left of the gate. Carry on in the same direction. Ignore the path leading downhill left into the field.

Keep on as the path you're on curves left and leads you to the corner of the field and a smaller 5 bar gate. Pass through the gap and walk down to the A25.

Taking your life in your hands, cross with care and walk up the tarmac track on the other side, passing the pumphouse immediately right.

You'll see farm buildings ahead. At the white farmhouse swing left 15 to 20 paces, then right, uphill following the public bridleway sign. This is the beginning of a slow gentle climb for about ½ mile.

Once you reach the crest of the hill, you're walking on level ground with open fields either side. When the path swings left into the corner of the field, walk through the gap in the holly at the corner into the adjoining left field.

Follow the obvious diagonal path across to Raikes Lane. Turn right about 15 paces along the lane, then left on to the Public Footpath which takes you past Raikes Farm.

You'll see a yellow arrow on the barn right. Walk along the farm track that runs between the 2 houses. Follow it as it swings sharp left. (Do not pass through either of the two gates into the fields.) There's another yellow arrow on the gate post right, (well part of one) as the track swings left.

This farm track leads you on a slight incline, back through the fields to the church at Sutton Abinger. Walk across a cattle grid, past a grand house and motte, then finally past Abinger Manor, right before you reach the church.

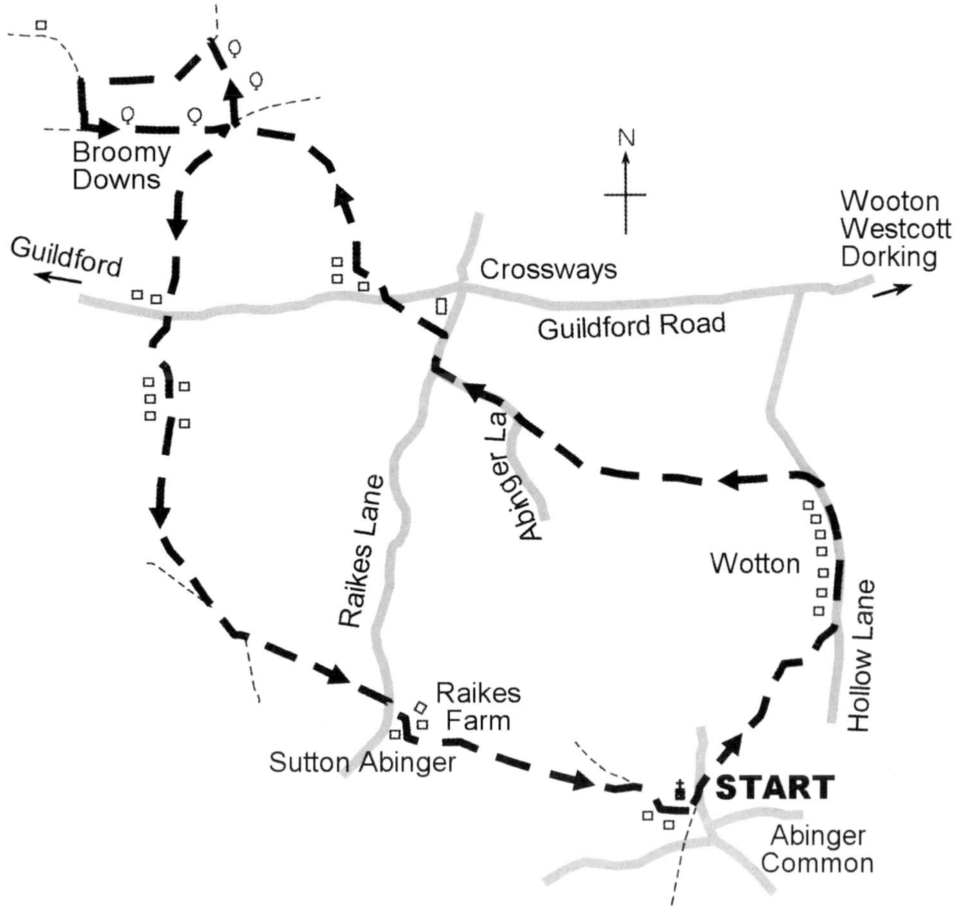

31. REIGATE HEATH TO GREENSAND WAY

Easy, 4 miles.
Best in drier conditions

Maps SSA P89 D5 OS SSA p117 D1
Start from the CP in Flanchford Road, just west of Reigate. It's about 1/4 mile from the A25, 5 mins walk at most from bus stop.

Walk back up Flanchford Road to the A25 to the corner next to the Black Horse pub. Cross the A25 and walk up Colley Lane. Ignore the turn off right to Pavillion cottages. You'll soon have views up to the North Downs. Mind the potholes while you're looking!

Cross the railway line and continue to a junction and cluster of houses. Turn left into The Clears. Just past Clears Farm left, you'll see a wooden footpath sign pointing right towards the North Downs. Follow it up a wide path between farm buildings and houses, then running between fields where it becomes a wide grassy swathe.

As you approach the tree line the path narrows and may be a bit overgrown in places. When you reach the tree line and a junction, just after the top corner of the left field, turn left. As you walk along this short section of the Pilgrims Way, you'll have views between the tree trunks south.

After passing through a small yew plantation you'll come to a junction and a wooden rail. Turn left downhill on to the public bridleway. This is a wide tree lined gravel path. When you reach the sealed lane, continue straight on down under the railway line. Then you'll have a short easy ascent past a few houses.

When you reach Willowdown Cottage, a charming whitewashed cottage right, turn right along the farm track. Just before you reach the house at the end of the track, turn hairpin left into the small grassy field. Follow the rough track through the grass, keeping more or less parallel with the boundary right. This path is not for bare legs when the grass and nettles are high. (Secateurs and a stick will be handy.)

Pass through the wooden gate into the well kept Rhododendron patch. (It is a Public Footpath). At the far end there's a metal gate between conifers into an allotment like area. At the end of this stretch, (at time of writing 5/7/99). there's a somewhat ancient stile. Keep straight on until you come to a metal kissing gate. Once through it, there's another wooden gate a few paces right.

If you look into the grounds of the two houses here you'll see a magnificent tree, possibly a cedar of some kind? Turn left back to Cliftons Lane, then right down to the A25, which you will hear. On reaching it, turn left along the footpath for 10 or so paces. Cross the A25 to the bridleway running parallel to the road.

Concentrate carefully on this next bit and watch the map closely, as there are many paths here. Turn right along the bridleway for about 150–200 yds when you'll reach a junction. There's a wooden bench under two trees and as you face it, there's a path 15–20 feet to right of it. Take this sandy path slightly down hill. Don't turn left or right but stay on it until you see the fairway through the trees.

Turn right and downhill on to a distinct well used bridleway, about 20–30 feet before the fairway, still in the trees. After 20–30 yards you'll come to a sandy vehicle track. You're close to the A25 and will hear it. Turn right along the track for about 12–15 paces, then take a narrow path off it to the left. You will quickly come to another gravelly vehicle track.

You'll see cars on the A25 here. Continue for another 15–20 paces along the narrow track which brings you out at a footpath sign, and a sliding rail stile (the most civilised we have come across), to your immediate left. (You're about 10 feet from the A25 here). Pass through it and follow the obvious path, with a field left and woods right.

Eventually you'll come to a wooden 2 step stile. Follow the well worn path across the grass and under the power lines. At the junction, turn left still inside the field. The path runs to the far end of the field, following close to the hedgerow right.

You'll finally come to a wooden gate. Pass through it to the wide track through the trees to the stream. At the tee junction, turn left and follow the path back to the edge of the golf course, a cottage left.

You'll see a path on the hill on the far side of the fairway. When there are no golfers, cross the fairway to the path. This is a public footpath, in fact it's part of the Greensand Way. This will lead you up towards the clubhouse and windmill.

On reaching the road that leads to the clubhouse, turn down it to Flanchford Road.

Cross and walk down the private road, (to Heathfield and Heathside.) When you're almost at the end, take the track left, leaving the sealed surface, and bringing you in 10–20 paces to cottages. Look for the narrow footpath to your right (still the Greensand Way) which runs between the houses, and brings you out, (after twists and turns) at Skimmington Castle pub.

Turn down hill, with cottages immediately left. As you draw level with a white cottage on your left at the bottom of the hill, you'll see a finger post and a path on your right. Follow the blue public bridleway sign. You're still on the Greensand Way, with the golf course left.

After 50 paces or so, at another short wooden finger post, turn left on to a less well defined track, passing two golf tees right, then moving into the trees. Follow your nose the short distance from here to the car park.

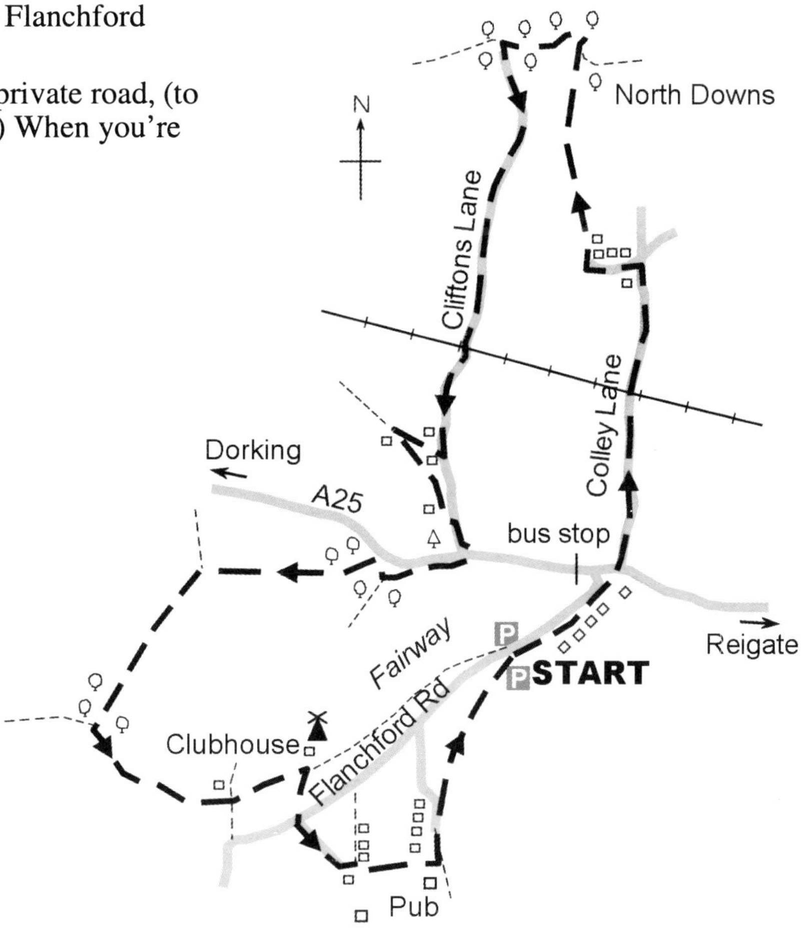

32. HOLMBURY ST MARY

Hilly, 4½ miles.

Try in opposite direction when wet.

Maps SSA P123 E1 OS SSA p155 C5
Start from the Holly Bush Tavern, Holmbury St Mary, or could be started from Friday Street CP. There's a regular bus service to Holmbury St Mary, a bus stop at the corner of Pitland Street and Horsham Road. Easy parking

Walk along the footpath on the same side of the road as the tavern, passing it on your right. At Pitland Street cross to the other side of Horsham Road. Turn left into Pasture Wood Road (part of the Greensand Way).

Just after passing Pasture wood cottage left, you'll see a Greensand Way path right. Ignore it. Walk on 50 yds or so to a second wooden finger post also right. This narrow but well defined path gently climbs and winds its way through Pasture Wood. Watch closely for the yellow arrows and follow them.

At a 3 way junction, an open field ahead, follow the yellow arrow sharp right. (there are also clear hand made signs on the trees, with arrows at time of writing). As you reach the top, the walking is more open with a variety of small trees, bracken and brambles.

At a wide green track, follow the yellow arrow left, then after 20 paces or so, cross a stile also marked with arrow. Walk left a few paces to a wide wooden gate. (There may be a Beware of Bull sign at certain times of year. We have passed him and his cows with no trouble at all. Don't panic! Keep to the right fence line.

At the top corner of the field, (there's another open field right). Go straight on, crossing an old but sturdy stile. You're now walking with a field right, woods left and holly and brambles to both sides. At a grassy open junction, follow the yellow arrow, passing between gorse brambles and ragwort to Leith Hill Road.

The path continues on the other side of the road, taking you downhill then crossing Abinger Bottom path. Then there's an easy climb and at the top, just after houses right, views left to Ranmore and St Barnabas spire.

Go on through the kissing gate into the field and walk down under power lines. At the end of field, walk up through woods to Leylands Lane. Turn left down the road. Immediately after Leylands Farm, take the footpath to left, an open field right

Turn right as you reach another open field. On reaching the corner of the field, you'll see a green public footpath sign pointing left. Follow it downhill, still on the edge of the same field. At a yellow arrow by a large tree, an obvious path leads you right, out of the field into woods.

As the path forks you'll see another green footpath sign pointing left. Walk down this soft leafy path which leads into a road with a sealed surface, passing Longfield Farm, and a pond and stream left.

Keep on downhill, passing cottages left. Swing right down Abinger Common Road until you reach the end of the last property left (St Johns). At this point turn right off the road onto a dirt bridleway, and under an ancient Yew. You'll see a wooden sign with SCC oak motif and Wotton Estate.

Follow this wide path, beside a small stream, and soon passing a wooden bridge on right. After 5–10 minutes you'll emerge at a sealed lane, and pass several cottages and the Stephan Langton pub.

Walk straight on down to the pond. Turn left up the road, and after about 50 paces, turn left a few yards to some steps and a path that runs parallel with the road. This takes you up to Friday Street CP.

If starting the walk at Friday Street car park Turn off A25, down Hollow Lane, turn hairpin left into Friday Street. CP is on R about a half mile along, before you go down hill to the pond.

At the CP, turn your back to the road and walk to the far right end. Look for a path that runs from the extreme right corner, There's a wooden sign next to it saying 'protect wildlife'. There's another path a little to left. Ignore it.

Follow this corner path along, then down into a dip. There is a junction of paths here. Travelling in the same direction, take the path that passes under the power lines, then up a slight incline. After about 8–10 minutes you'll reach Hollow Lane. Cross it and go straight on, past a metal gate towards Pasture Wood Cottage. Cross a second road, (an old red phone box to your right), and continue straight on along the public footpath.

Soon after the fences either side end, the path dips, then reaches a junction. Ignore the path running left to right and walk straight on up a gentle incline. (There is a path parallel up to right to keep you out of mud.) On top this becomes a wide grassy path with a birch plantation right. There are occasional breaks in the plantation with views of the North Downs.

When the path starts to descend, go into your lowest gear and prepare for a knee creaking steep stretch! There's a wire strand fence right which can be used to steady yourself, but not to take your full weight.

At the bottom of this short sharp stretch, turn left along a wide flat easy track with rhododendrons either side. It may be muddy in places, but the edges should be ok.

When you come to a junction, with a field ahead and a farm track coming down from the left, turn right onto it. This leads you past a charming lodge on the right, over the stream back in to Holmbury St Mary. Turn left and return to bus stop or car.

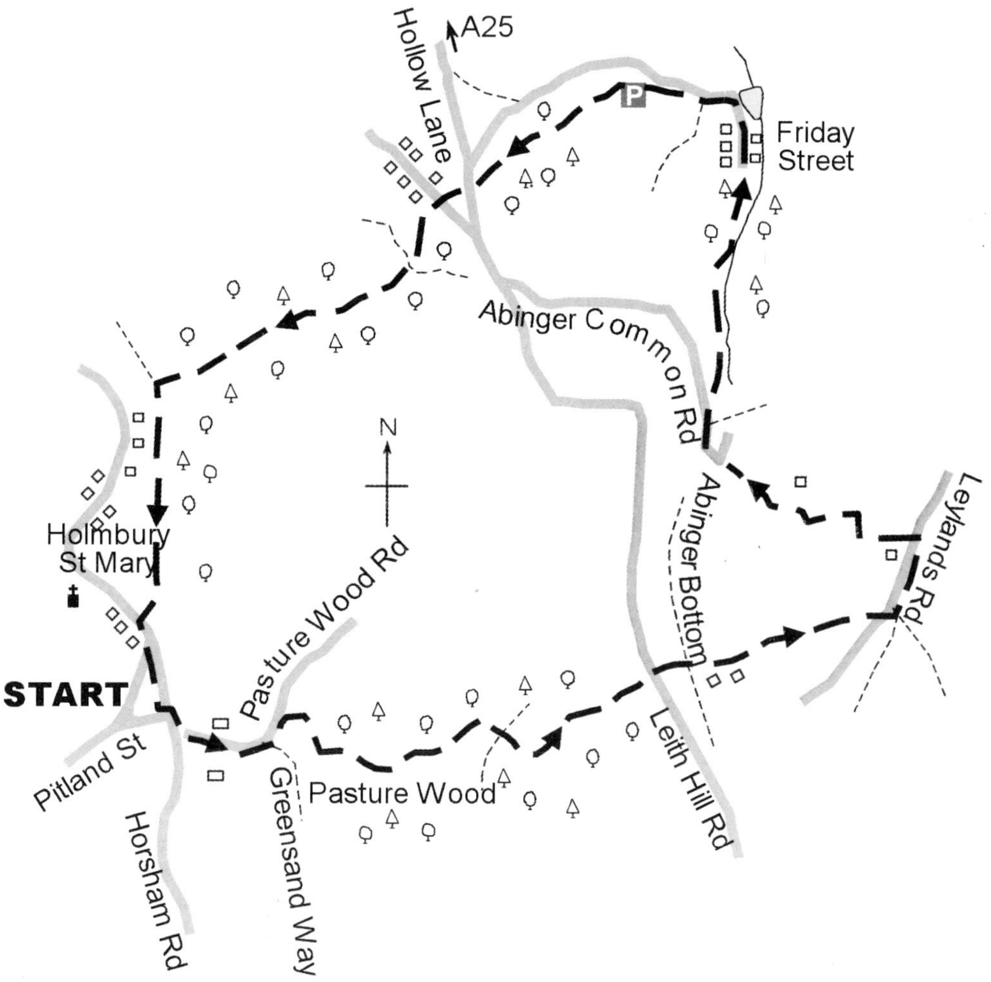

33. BETCHWORTH, BUCKLAND, PILGRIMS WAY, BROCKHAM
Easy, 5 miles

Maps SSA P107 D1 OS SSA p137 E8
Start at the church at Betchworth. There is no bus service. You could start the walk at Buckland or at Betchworth Station at Pebblehill Road. There is easy but limited street parking in Church Street.

Cross The Street into Wonham Lane, passing the Dolphin Inn left. After 10–20 yds there's a footpath left, which runs up and alongside a field to Sandy Lane. Continue on along Wonham Lane to the Wonham Manor gate house.

About 10 yds further on turn left through a gate onto a bridleway. Walk up the gentle incline and follow your nose, keeping to this path and passing through gates when they occur. It soon levels out, and once through the trees, you'll have views up to the North Downs and fields either side of you. It's a wide path, with a few muddy patches, mostly avoidable, unless it's been very wet.

At a junction with Pilgrim Cottage right, turn left up Dungates Lane, past Holly Lodge. Walk up to the A25, passing the shops and PO at Buckland. Cross to the pond on the other side and keep to the footpath on the left, passing The Towered Barn. Keep on down Rectory Lane,

When you reach Glebe Cottage left, turn left before it, following the footpath sign. Go through the gate into the open field, and keep straight on in the direction you've been moving, passing a small corner of field right.

Keep more or less to the right hedge line. You'll see ahead an old oak and right of it a ground level bridge, with a disused gate, right of it.

Cross the bridge and follow the well worn narrow path up the centre of the field towards the North Downs. (There's a brick house a little way off right.)

Heading for power poles, you'll come to two steps and a metal kissing gate. Go through and turn left along a tunnel of hazelnut trees. This runs parallel with the railway line, to a level crossing.

When you reach the crossing at Pebblehill Road, cross this busy road with care, Then turn right crossing the railway line. Walk up the elevated footpath. Pass Betchworth Lodge then turn left at The Coombe.

At the next junction turn left past new cottages, with The Old Studio left. This leads you onto the (NDW). You'll climb gently until you come to a wooden gate with a sign, 'Heavy Plant Crossing—Caution.' There's a landfill site right.

Cross and continue on the other side. You're now walking on chalk which is very slippery when wet. After 10–20 yds, there's a clearing left with views of tower and beyond. 10–20 yds further from here, look down and you'll see a lower path Pilgrims Way, through the yews. Keep an eye on it.

After another 50 yds or so, at a slight dip, turn a hairpin left, leaving the NDW. This gives you a comfortable descent to the lower path. Continue west, on this path as it dips and climbs, following the fence line.

Eventually it will lead you to The Limeworks, a new (1999) brick cottage on your left. There are a couple of sign boards giving you some history. Then swing left through a narrow wooden gate, onto a short permissive footpath, leaving the path you were on.

Follow this lane to cottages right. At corner turn left down Chalkpit Lane. (The cottages here were originally built for miners.) Continue on, crossing the railway line again, and walk down to the A25, with Stoney Croft Tarn on left corner.

Go straight across to the footpath sign on the other side and follow the path down to Brockham Lane. The playing fields left are NT property and intended for sports only, Therefore, walk along the footpath at the side of the field, then left into Kiln Lane.

Look for a footpath right once you've passed the houses, Cross the lane to the Public Footpath sign and walk up the path with a hedge right and field left. At the top of the rise look back for a lovely view.

Follow this path as it slowly curves left, following the fence line. At a junction, go straight on, keeping the river right, and passing back gardens of several houses. (Spindleberrys here in October/ November.) Keep on this path back to the church.

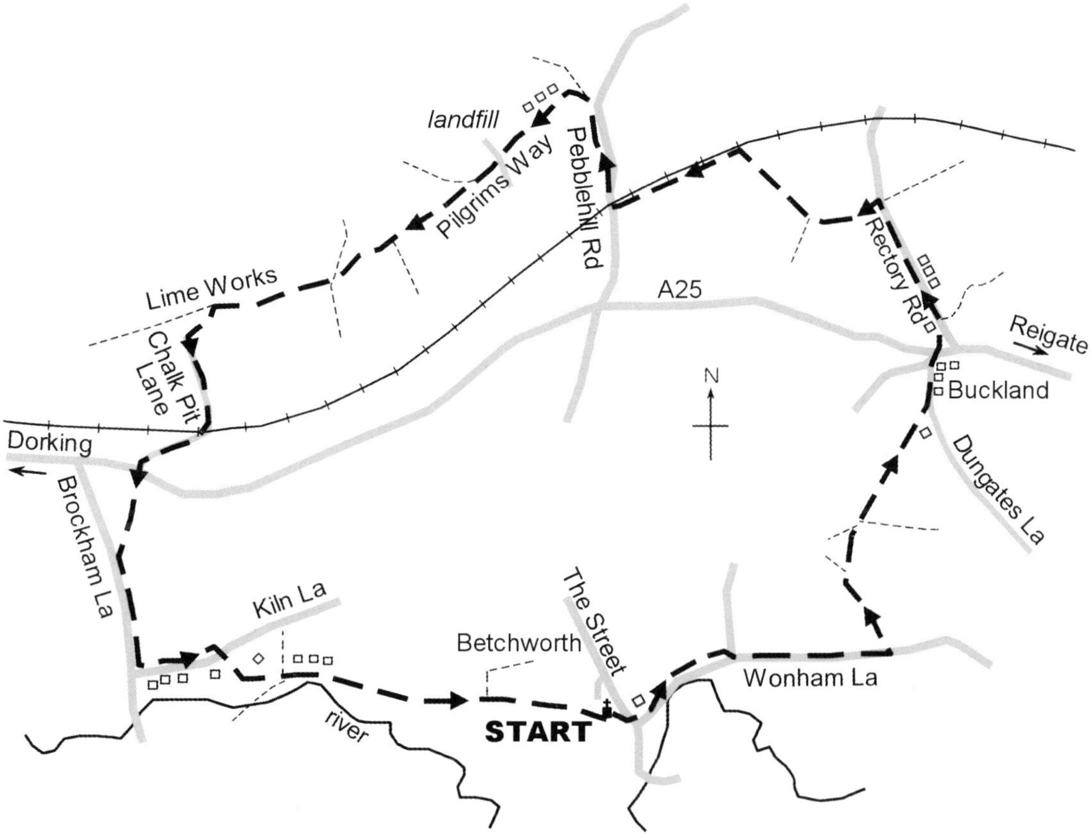

34. WILD WEST OF RANMORE

Hilly, 5 miles

Maps SSA F5 P85 OS SSA p113 F1
Start Ranmore West NT CP. There are two car parks on Ranmore Common Road. Heading up Ranmore Road from Dorking, ignore the first car park on your left at the top of the hill. There's a second car park with a donation box, almost exactly a mile on, also on your left.

With your back to the road, turn right out of the car park and turn left immediately through a wooden barrier onto a wide winding gravel track. As the track straightens out, you'll pass a wooden platform in a tree left, signed 'Not For Public Use'.

At the first junction, still on level ground, turn right (west) onto a wide path with a fairly good surface. Mud can usually be avoided. As soon as the path veers noticeably right, (at a green wooden Forestry Commission sign), look out for a path on left. This stretch, still running west, may be grassier and muddier.

At the next Tee junction, turn left onto a wide track through the trees. You'll soon begin a gentle descent, the path veering right through beech trees, to join the NDW. You'll pass a wooden sign board right. There's soon a steep drop to your left and yew trees.

At a wooden 5 bar gate, a bunker/ pill box left, pass through the gate and continue downhill, leaving the NDW. You'll soon have views left. Beware of an enticing little path that runs parallel left, outside the tree line. It's on chalk and is like an ice rink when wet.

At the bottom of the hill, when you'll come to a junction, turn right. The path soon curves left to a gate, then leads you across a bridge over the railway line. Walk straight on down towards Park Farm. At a four way junction, pass the farm driveway and turn right, passing between farm buildings.

On your left now is Wotton Estate, right, a fence and field. Follow this path until you reach the road, (White Down Lane). Turn right and cross the railway bridge. Now walk a short way up this busy back road.

Just before the first corner you'll see a wooden barrier and a footpath sign on the right. Keep on up the road as it swings left then right up hill again. About 150 yards from this second corner there's a tall finger post with a public footpath sign on your left. Watch for it as it's not too obvious.

Follow the path left, then up hill past a wooden gate left and another pill box right. You'll quickly reach the NDW path, a 5 bar gate left. Look to the right for a wooden finger post. Take about 5 steps to the right on the NDW then follow another public footpath up hill again. It's steepish at first but soon levels out, following a fence left, with lovely views.

At the next T junction you'll reach a wide track running left and right. Turn right on to it. It's easy walking from here with views right.

The path finally leaves the cleared area and turns left into the woods. Stay on this wide track, keeping to the left side until you reach an iron railing, fencing in a reservoir.

At the Tee junction at the end of the railings, turn right along the vehicle track. Follow this to a wooden barrier and White Down Lane again. You can cross straight over here, but there's often a mud hole on the other side. Instead, turn left a few feet then cross to another wide wooden barrier.

Follow this wide track which curves left then is more or less straight to Ranmore Common road. Just before you reach the road, (you'll hear traffic) you'll reach a junction.(This last bit is a damp/muddy spot) Turn right, then immediately left 'til you reach the road, a brick cottage on the other side.

Cross, turn right and walk 50 yds or so. Then turn left at low wooden posts. (For short cut walk along the bridle way on this side of the road—muddy!—back to the car park.) Otherwise follow the diagonal grassy swathe, bracken either side. There are a lot of paths here.

Keep on the main wide stretch. At a short wooden post with blue arrow, keep right up a slight incline. At an open area tend to veer right. The path follows the bracken on the right. At a junction take the middle route. As long as you are more or less keeping to a straight diagonal, all paths lead to Rome.

If you veer too far right you'll come to Stonyrock Road sooner than intended. No worries! Ideally you should pass to the left of a car park at the road side, with a wooden post with a blue arrow on it at the corner of the car park. Keep on to a junction with a house, path and road.

Cross the road and walk down the track past the 'No Horses' sign through a dark tunnel of trees. This brings you out at Hogden Lane, a cottage left. Turn right up the lane until in sight of Ranmore Common Road (20–30 yds). Turn left onto a wide track for 50 yds, then right between wooden posts to CP.

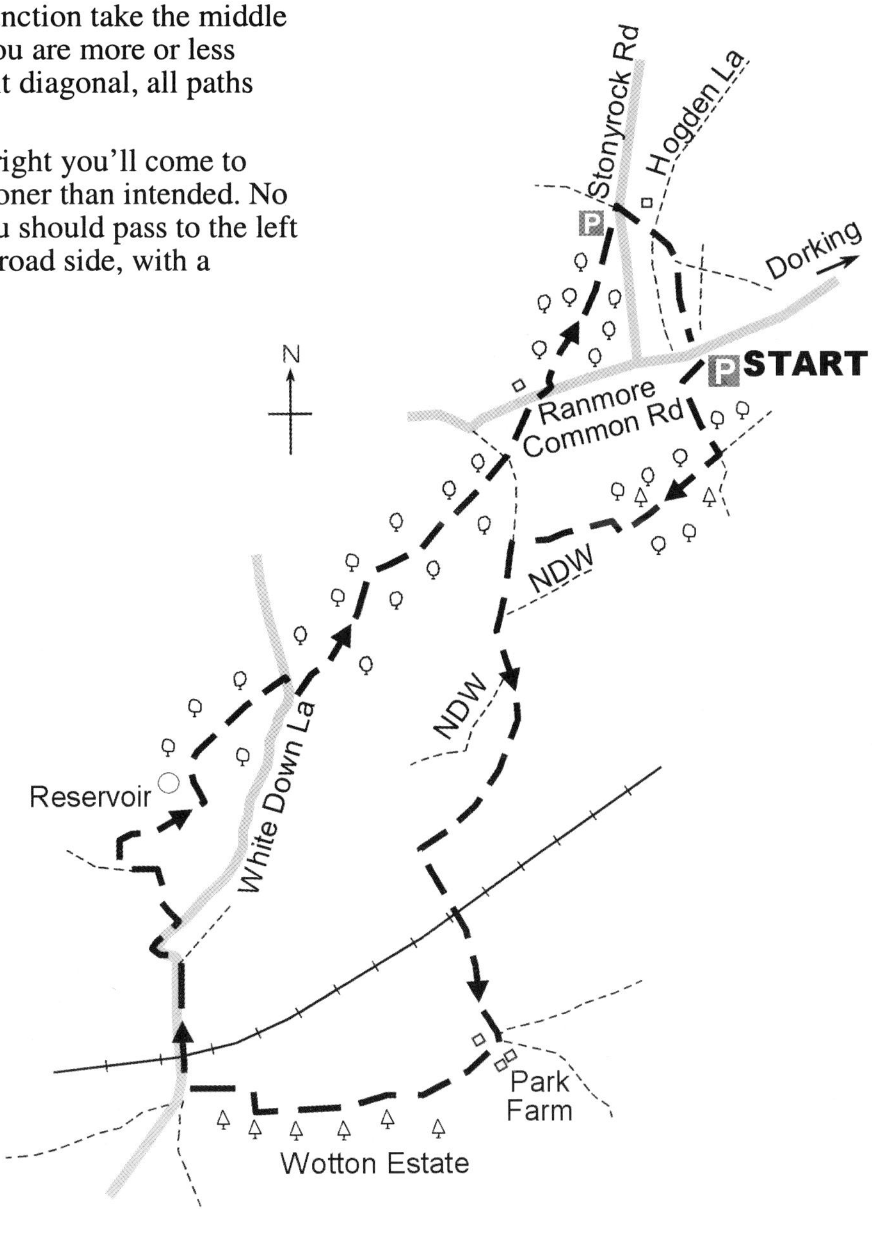

35. GOMSHALL, NORTH DOWNS WAY, SILENT POOL, SHERE

Hills, 5+ miles.

Dry or damp weather

Maps SSA P 103 E3 OS SSA p133 D4

Start at Gomshall. There's a train station as well as bus services. On weekends you can park at Gomshall station, or other times near the corner of Highview and Queen Street.

You could also start this walk at several other points along the way—West Hangar car park, Silent Pool car park, or Shere.(see map) However, I find this is the most pleasing arrangement, and have selected paths and tracks to give you the best possible walking in damp or dry conditions.

Starting on the A25, at the Old Mill, walk west, past the Compass Pub, then cross the A25 and walk up Colekitchen Lane.

When you reach the 'Beech Trees, Clock House, Round Down Cottage' sign on your right, turn left into Kingswood Hanger, signed to Liddy Fields. Take the right fork up hill when you reach Liddyfields drive. This is a steady climb so take your time. It's worth it. Walk on up passing Hillside Lodge.

When you come to a T junction, a bridleway running left and right, turn left. Ignore the footpath with a wooden barrier leaving the bridleway immediately left. Keep on up the bridleway as it turns up hill. You'll notice after a short distance another path leading off left, passing through a wide wooden barrier. Ignore this also. (The going is much easier from here.)

About 200 yds from this point, you'll reach another Tee junction and a well defined surfaced path, The North Downs Way. There's a wooden finger post with blue and white arrows, signed NDW. Turn left along the NDW. No more climbing.

At the next junction, a raised concrete reservoir left, keep straight on. A little further on, you'll pass through a wooden barrier and there'll be a farm right, a postbox on the corner of the last building you pass.

Ignore two tracks left and swing right with the main farm track (still the NDW tho' lack of signs here). As soon as this track starts to turn the corner to left, leave it, continuing straight on along the NDW, now a narrower path. (At time of writing there's a pile of rubble for surfacing at this corner so you can't miss it.)

When you reach a road, Combe Lane, cross blind bend with care, and turn right a few steps, then left again at the corner still following the NDW. There's another reservoir, ground level, right.

You'll quickly come to another road, Staple Lane. Cross and walk through West Hanger CP on the other side, continuing along the NDW. This is a muddier stretch during wet conditions, but most is avoidable. At the next junction take the right fork, still on the NDW.

Very soon now, you'll reach another junction and a tall signpost pointing left down to Silent Pool. There's also a short post saying public footpath, with a yellow arrow. Leave the NDW and descend. It's steepish but not too slippery unless there's been rain for a week or more.

About half way down the field on your right, as the path starts to level out, there's a stumpy thick post with green markings left. Turn left at this post, down steps to the pools.

There are two pools. You can walk either side of the first, then keep right of the second. This is a perfect spot for a break if it's quiet.

Continue down to the A25. Cross and turn left (east). At the A248 cross to the footpath behind the hedge then turn right towards Albury. Turn left up a track before reaching the field with the church. This leads to a 5 bar gate and stile. Cross and follow the well worn path across the field.

Cross the stile at the far side into the woods. This leads you down to another field with a dip in it. Continue straight on, heading for a pine forest. Walk through the trees down to a lane. Turn right, cross the stream then turn left through Vicky's gate. Follow the stream until you reach the next ford.

Turn right here before the cottages, into Willow Walk. Walk up 5 steps then left, then right onto a drive. (Hope you're good at your lefts and rights!)

At the fork keep right up hill, which takes you on to a narrow footpath between the houses down to Pilgrims Close. Turn left down Pathfields to Shere Lane.

Cross and walk up The Spinning Walk past the old surgery and on up to the bridleway. If you've time to explore Shere, you could turn left where Spinning Walk meets the bridle way. This leads down to the church and village. You can't go wrong from here when you want to head for home.

Once on the bridleway continue straight on. At Gravelpits Farmhouse turn left on to main drive, passing Highlands left. Walk down Gravelpits Lane back to the corner of Highview and Queen Street, and return to your starting place.

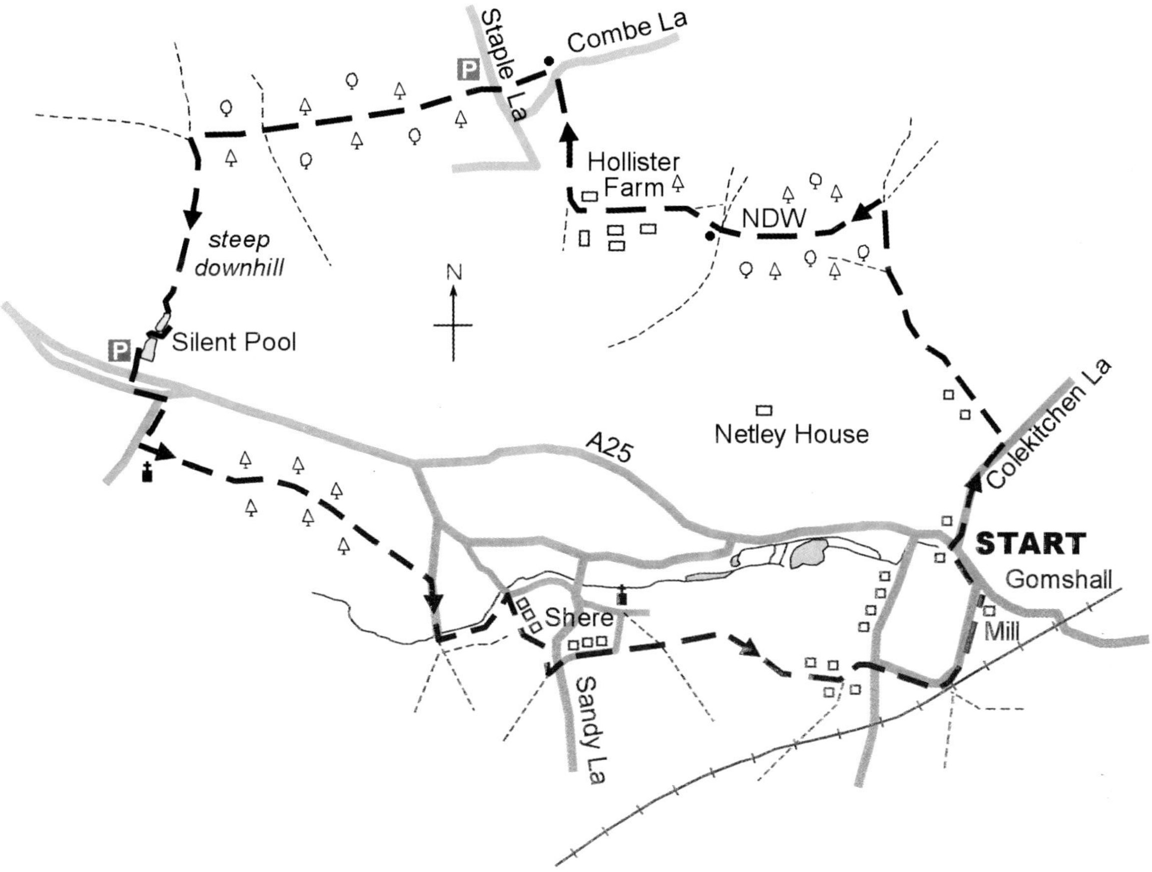

36. SHERE HEATH, BLACKHEATH & ALBURY HEATH

Easy—undulating 4½ miles.
A great walk for all weathers.

Maps SSA P103 D4 OS SSA p133 A2
Start Shere Heath CP just south-west of Shere.

If travelling by public transport, you may have to catch a bus to Shere and walk the short distance from there to the CP. Driving from the A25, turn into Shere and drive south through the middle of the village. This road becomes Sandy Lane. Turn right just before the railway line. The CP is 2 or 3 hundred yards along on your left.

Facing the road, turn left onto worn track across grass, parallel with, and about 20 ft away from road. (Every now and then, turn and look back as you will retrace your steps here at the end of the walk).

The path leads you into trees, through bracken and nettles, sandy under foot. Turn left at junction and walk on down to Tee junction. Turn left across railway line, then turn right down sealed lane, the cottages left.

Keep straight on as sealed lane is replaced by sandy byway, into a shady tunnel of trees. As you reach a building right, (Ponds Farm) look for a stile before it, on the right. Cross the stile, the path running between a fence left and brick block wall right. Then cross another stile and walk on along Ponds Lane.

Turn left at Brook Lane Then left again along Brook Hill. Immediately past Brook Cottage there's a red phone box and just after it a footpath, running parallel with the road. Walk up this path. It brings you out at corner of a road with signs, Windy Ridge, Glendale etc in front of you.

The footpath continues again just after Farley Lodge, a shady walk under tall conifers. Once again the path emerges at the road, a caravan Park left. Follow the road (August Lane), walking past the grassy triangle left. Once past the houses right, at a Hurtwood control sign, turn right down a vehicle track.

At a junction with houses left, follow the footpath sign left. (Do not continue on the sandy bridleway right). You'll pass several cottages left. Then the track becomes a path into the trees.

When you reach an intersection of a bridleway and the footpath you're on, turn right up the sandy bridleway onto a plateau. Concentrate carefully here. Go straight on now, looking for a level sandy stretch with a short finger post on your R, (just after a track off to your left).

Turn right at the finger post (bridleway sign). The post is under an oak and a pine at time of writing and the path leads you downhill, on a gully like track.

This may be muddy when it's very wet but any mud should be avoidable. You'll pass some houses left then the path will emerge on a sandy vehicle track, Blackheath Lane. There's a footpath coming in from the right at this corner.

Keep straight on down the lane. This is easy sheltered walking down into the valley. You'll cross a bridge over the stream. Look for a stile on right now, into the field, just before an arched railway bridge.

Once in the field, keep to the flat valley floor. Ignore the worn cattle track up the bank and keep close-ish to fence right, passing a fish farm right. You'll then pass a farm cottage left and come to a stile in the left corner of the field.

Cross and turn left, then follow this farm track as it takes you to the right, between farm buildings and under power lines.

At a T junction with a Public Bridleway sign pointing right, turn left uphill on a sealed track (barely a hill), passing under railway arch.

Just before you get to the top of the hill (just as you can see a sports hut ahead) you'll see 2 paths on right, up the bank. Take either. The second is a bridleway so may be chewed up. Once up the bank aim to turn left on to an unsealed vehicle track.

This leads past a CP on right, and Albury Heath sports ground left. Walk straight on to the road, and a sign, 'Woodside'. Cross to path on other side and go straight on. You'll soon see cottages ahead. A grassy path leads you to the first 2 left.

On reaching the cottages, turn right passing all the cottages on your left. This is the back of Little London. The last cottage will be Fircroft. Walk on turning left at a brick building with no windows.

Walk down the track to a concrete hump. Just before the hump, look for a footpath left. (the sign's obscured at time of writing). Turn down this winding path into the trees and follow it down to the road. There's a sign here on your left 'Little London'.

Now either go under the railway arched bridge and turn left into Ponds Lane, retracing your steps to the CP. Or if you'd prefer, walk up Dark Lane through Little London and past the pub (See map for alternate finish.)

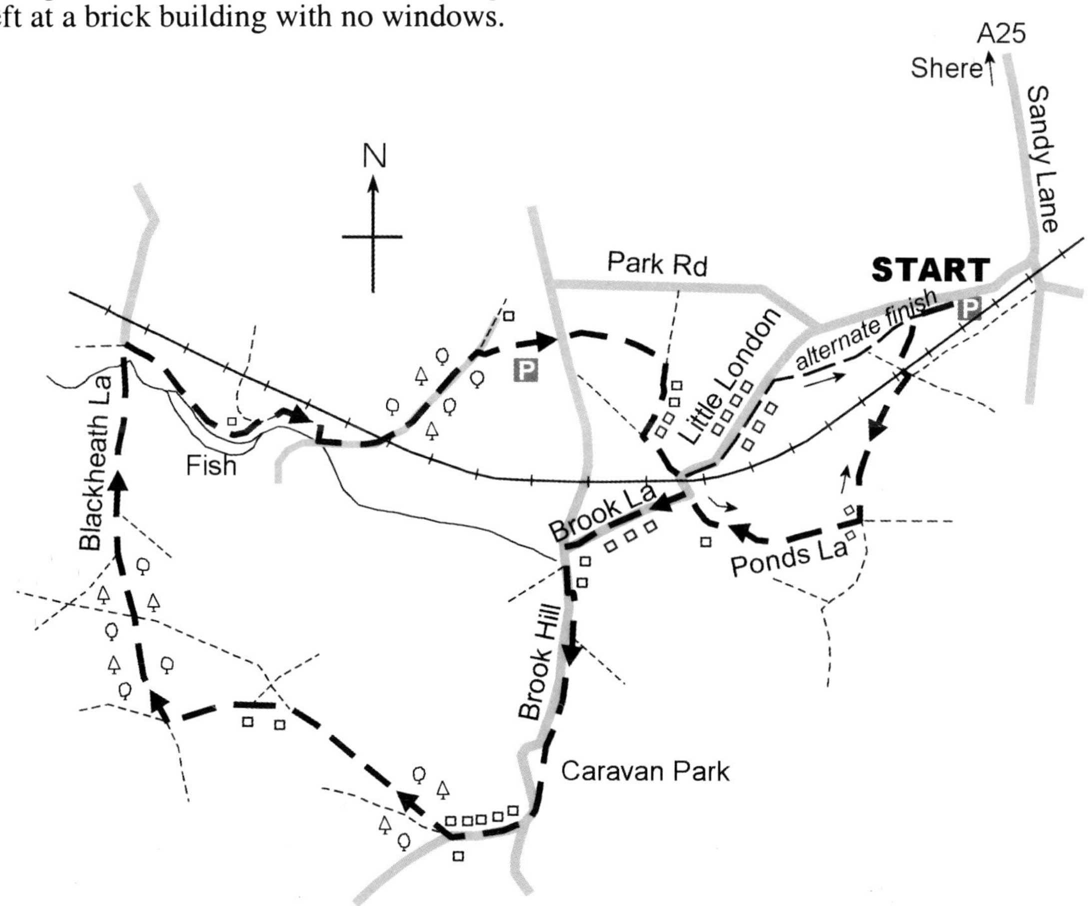

37. GOMSHALL, LITTLE LONDON & SHERE

Easy undulating 3¾ miles.
Perfect for a balmy evening.
Good underfoot all weathers

Maps SSA P103 E3 OS SSA p133 C4
Start at the corner of High View and Queen Street, Gomshall. There's a bus stop here for Tillingbourne Buses, or limited parking along High View. There's a train station at Gomshall.

Cross Queen Street and walk along Gravelpits Lane. (see public bridleway post) At a corner where track swings right, don't! Continue straight on, keeping left of Gravelpits Farmhouse, and passing tennis courts right. The path climbs gently, taking you over a railway bridge (which you might not notice) and then between two fields, a wire fence either side.

When you reach the end of the right field, turn right along a well worn track, a fence right and trees left. (There is a finger post, but arrow faded at time of writing.) Follow the path up to the road passing cottages.

At Hook Lane turn right 20–30 paces then left down public footpath, a fingerpost on RHS. Keep to the fence on right, over stile, then between two fields, then across another stile to Houndhouse Road. Lovely views.

Cross the lane and walk 30–40 paces left to Parklands Farm sign. Turn right down this byway, passing cottages left. When you reach the corner with the railway gate right, turn left, passing more cottages left.

The byway soon starts to look like a sandy path—a tunnel between two banks. Just as you've descended from a slight rise, you'll come to Ponds Farm right. Turn right here, before the buildings, crossing a stile, and walking a short stretch between a retaining wall right, and a farm fence left.

Cross a second stile into Ponds Lane and follow it to Brook Lane. At Brook Lane turn right under the railway bridge then immediately left at the Little London sign, along a footpath.

This path climbs gently as it winds away from the road, and emerges at a concrete speed bump, a pretty cottage left. Turn right along the track to a red brick building with no windows right.

Straight after this building turn right again on to Heath Lane (not signed). At a junction, walk straight on passing Yew Tree Cottage right. Keep on along this bumpy track keeping cottages to right until you reach Park Road.

Turn right along verge to first corner then cross Park Road with South Lodge on left. There are 3 footpaths here. One immediately left through green gates next to South Lodge. Take the second through kissing gate.

This leads you down a lovely open grassy path, all the way to the ford at the west edge of Shere. Don't cross the stream. Turn right through Vicky's gate and follow the stream into Shere Village, via Lower Street.

Cross the main road veering right into The Square, heading for the church. A perfect opportunity to look around, have a drink etc

Continue on along Church Lane, past Church Cottage right (spot the hearts?). Turn right immediately after Church Hill Road through a wooden gate, up a public footpath. At the Tee junction at the top end of this narrow path, turn left back to Gomshall, with views left.

When you reach a corner with Gravelpits Farm right, you'll have your bearings for the end of the walk.

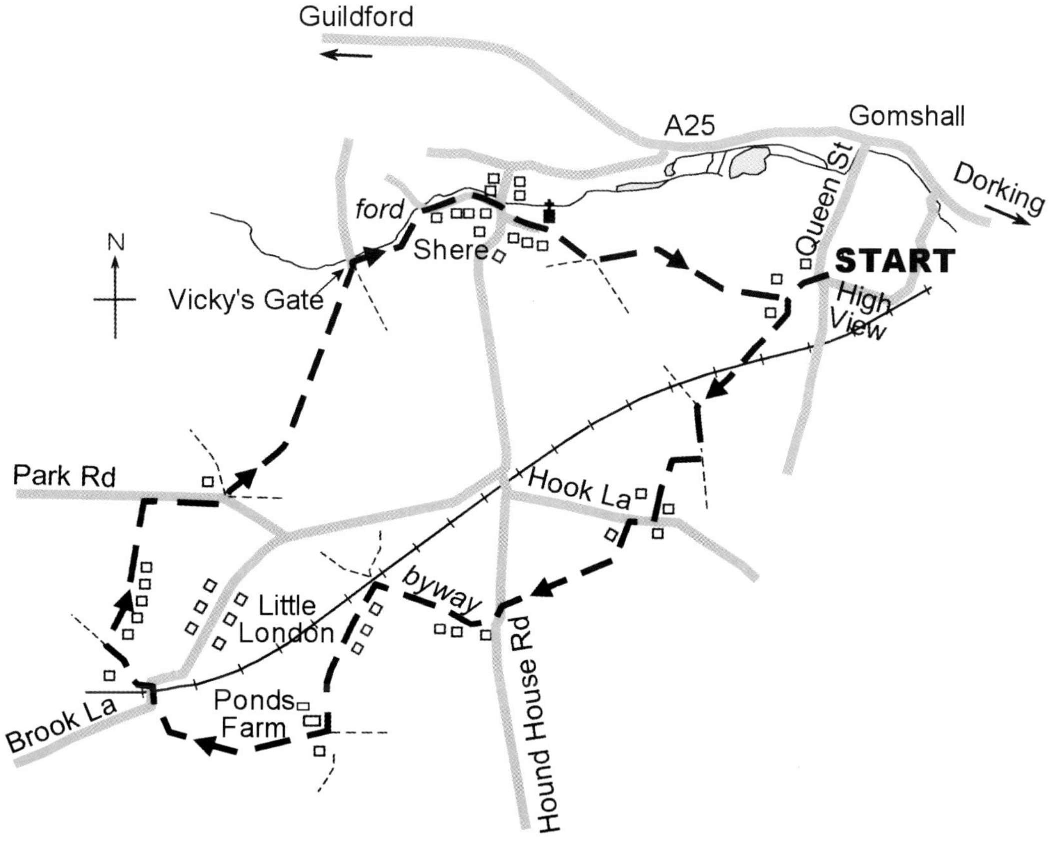
Guildford
A25
Gomshall
Dorking
N
ford
Shere
Queen St
START
High View
Vicky's Gate
Park Rd
Hook La
byway
Little London
Ponds Farm
Brook La
Hound House Rd

38. SILENT POOL TO OLD PARISH CHURCH

Easy, 4¼–5 miles.
Good underfoot wet or dry

Maps SSA P 102 C2 OS SSA p132 D5
Start Silent Pool CP

There is a bus stop right by CP By car. Drive along the A25 heading west towards Guildford. The CP is just the other side of Shere. At dual carriageway, move to middle lane, slow, and you can turn right almost immediately across A25 and left into CP.

Cross the A25, and turn left (east). At the A248 (Albury Street) cross to the footpath behind the hedge then turn right away from A25. Just before reaching the field with the church left, you'll come to a footpath running left and right.

Cross the A248 again to the gate and stile on the other side. Ten paces or so, cross a second stile into an open field. Follow the obvious path up a slight incline to the next stile. Once over this, you're walking through light woods with many new plantings (yr 2000).

If you keep an eye left you'll see a Quarry warning. At the entrance to the Quarry, cross the wide concrete drive, giving way to traffic. Walk on through more woods and onto a level farm track.

You'll reach a wide green gate with a stile, and on the other side you'll pass Timbercroft Cottage left. The left side of this farm track is sandy and easy walking.

You'll finally reach Water Lane Cottages left. A few feet past the drive entrance you'll see 'the welcoming committee' at the steps. Turn left and walk down Water Lane to the A248 again.

Cross and turn left along the footpath which takes you round the bend, past Weston Farm of Albury Estate. Turn R after Clive Lodge up Church Lane.

Keep straight on into Blackheath Lane, up a gentle ascent. Eventually you'll emerge from tree cover into the open with a large open barn right. At the top of the hill, in fact just over the crest you'll see a bridleway left.

EXTRA LOOP FOR LONGER ROUTE
Ignore bridleway left. Take the footpath that runs beside the road right, to the bottom of the hill. Walk under railway bridge, then look for a footpath sign on your left, just before the stream. This takes you into a field.

Once in the field, keep to the flat valley floor. Ignore the worn cattle track up the bank and keep close-ish to the fence right, passing a fish farm right. **Do not cross the stream at any point**. You'll then pass a farm cottage left and come to a stile in the left corner of the field.

Cross and turn left, then follow this track as it takes you to the right between farm buildings and under power lines.

At a T junction with a public bridleway sign pointing right, turn left up hill, on a sealed track (barely a hill), under a railway arch

As you get to the top of the hill you will see a sports hut ahead right. Keep straight on up this track, passing the sports hut. This brings you out near the junction of New Road and Park Road, a cottage immediately left and the Albury Heath sports ground right.

SHORTER ROUTE
Leave the farm track and follow the bridleway left up to a wide green gate. The sandy track now levels out. Keep an ear out for horses as it's a good stretch for a gallop. Any puddles are easily avoidable.

After a section that's slightly downhill you'll reach a gate part way across the track, a chicken wire fence right. At the junction just past this gate take the right track. You'll see cars and a building through the trees right.

Keep on along the sandy eroded bridleway, crossing a drive and a little further on crossing another even more distinct vehicle track. This eventually brings you out near the junction of New Road and Park Road, a cottage immediately left and the Albury Heath sports ground right.

ROUTES MERGE AGAIN

Walk to the side of New Road and turn right and cross to the far corner of New Road and Park Road. Take the diagonal path that runs to a cleared heath area, with 3 cottages in view ahead. Swing left on to the wide sandy path that takes you to Heath Lane. Turn left and walk to Park Road.

Turn right along grass verge and walk to corner, with South Lodge on the other side. Cross and go through the small green gate next to the lodge. This is a public footpath. Should any one appear and try to deter you, politely take no notice. If they ask are you going to the church say yes. You are.

You will quickly reach a wide green gate. About 10 paces before it look for a yellow arrow pointing left. Follow the yellow arrows (not many) all the way to the church. There are many paths here on Albury estate. Most are private and well signed. Some yellow arrows are a little hard to spot but they are there.

The path finally curves right and downhill with a lovely view of the church before you reach it. Once through the gate and on to the grass, it's well worth a closer look. Walking out along the church drive.

At Park Lodge turn R then walk straight up the A248 to the A25. For a safer crossing, walk left 50 yds or so along the A25, as the junction of the 2 roads is a busy and speedy one. Take a look at the pools, only a minute from CP. A massive amount of work has been done to restore them to great beauty.

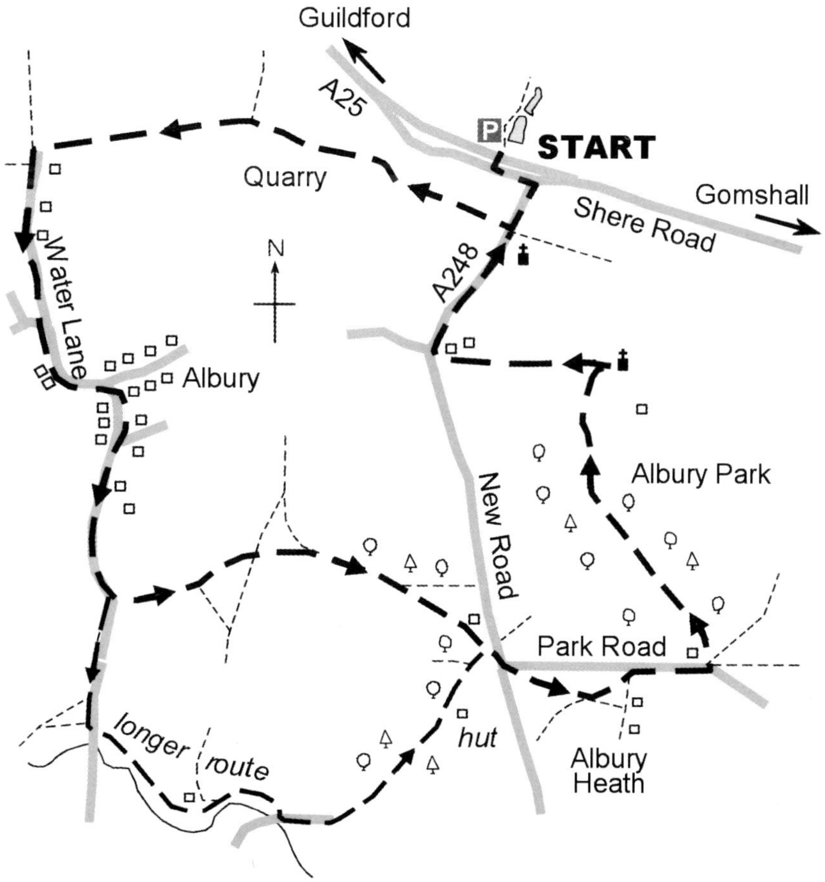

39. RANMORE, DENBIES, TANNERS HATCH YOUTH HOSTEL

4 or 5 miles.
Beautiful any time of year.
Good underfoot in wet weather.

Maps SSA P 86 A.5 OS SSA p114 C1
Start at Ranmore East NT CP.

Turn east and walk along the grass out of the CP and past cottages right. Then cross Ranmore Common Road and walk past 'The Old post Office'. (the only cottage on left.)

Continue walking along left edge of road toward the Parish Church, St Barnabus. There's a footpath through the grass on both sides of the road from the church. At the end of this straight stretch, as road swings left, walk straight on passing Denbies right, and continuing along the NDW .

Only a short distance from Denbies you'll come to a junction where the NDW swings right. Follow it. This quickly brings you to another junction just down the hill a little. Turn left, still keeping to the NDW. You'll soon pass through some huge green metal gates, with wonderful views on a clear day, right and ahead down over the vineyard and Dorking.

Soon after passing through second metal gates, the track starts to curve left. and then for a while light woodland obscures the view. Through a gap at four way junction, you look directly down to the Denbies Vineyard and buildings. Keep on the NDW, still heading in the same direction. The track curves right, then left, a view to the top of Box Hill right.

As the track curves right downhill you'll see a public footpath wooden finger post on the corner pointing left. Turn left along this track (instead of continuing on the NDW curving downhill right) soon passing a couple of houses and tennis courts up left. At the end of the wooden rail fence left, walk straight on along a narrow path that starts where fence ends. After 30 or 40 paces this brings you to a stile. Cross into the field and follow the power poles that lie straight ahead. At the third pole veer left slightly to the fence line, stile and gate.

Cross the stile, (somewhat chewed at time of writing) and walk along the narrow path beside the fence. At the far end breath in, and pass through a lethal looking stile into an open field. Keep to the fenceline right.

Cross the stile beside the wide wooden gate, into Ranmore Common Road again. Turn downhill to Chapel Lane. Turn left along the lane a few feet then enter the field on your right.

This is now NT property and it's permitted to walk along the boundary inside the field, parallel to the road. It will become an official permissive path later in 2001. 300–400 yards along you'll come to gates left and right. Turn left through lower gate and cross Chapel Lane again and follow the 'Bagden Farm' and Youth Hostel signs.

Walk past a farmhouse right then a low farm building. There's a bridleway sign here pointing right, but ignore it. Walk on, open fields left and right and soon Old Dene left.

On a corner at a wide wooden NT gate, turn right through the smaller gate, into the field, on to the bridleway. (No sign saying bridleway at time of writing.) Follow the obvious worn track across the grass, passing a solitary tree, to the next gate.

Go through and walk on to the next junction, taking the right path. After a short distance, there's another junction. Turn right again, walking almost parallel but a little higher than the tree line. You can still see the field below.

For a while the track ascends gently, then levels out. This is very easy walking and firm under foot.

As you reach some Yew trees right, you're almost at the youth hostel. This last 100 yds or so is mucky and you may be able to avoid the mud if you follow a vague path down right under the Yews to a parallel path below.

After the YH ignore the path that runs along beside the split rail fence. Turn up to left, quickly coming to another junction. If you'd like a shorter walker on a firm path with a slow ascent keep on the left track. If you'd like a 5 mile walk take the right track, which will be slightly muddy in places but not bad.

Follow the blue bridleway arrow right. You'll come to a corner with a junction and a split rail fence left. Stay on the track as it curves right, then slowly curves left again. Now you have an easy ascent, for about half a mile, (10–15 mins)

At the next junction with a split rail fence up the slope left and a post with a blue arrow (public bridleway), turn left up through the barrier in the rail fence and follow this diagonal path to Ranmore Common Road. It will be muddy in places, but the worst should be avoidable.

Turn left along side of Ranmore Common Road, back to the CP.

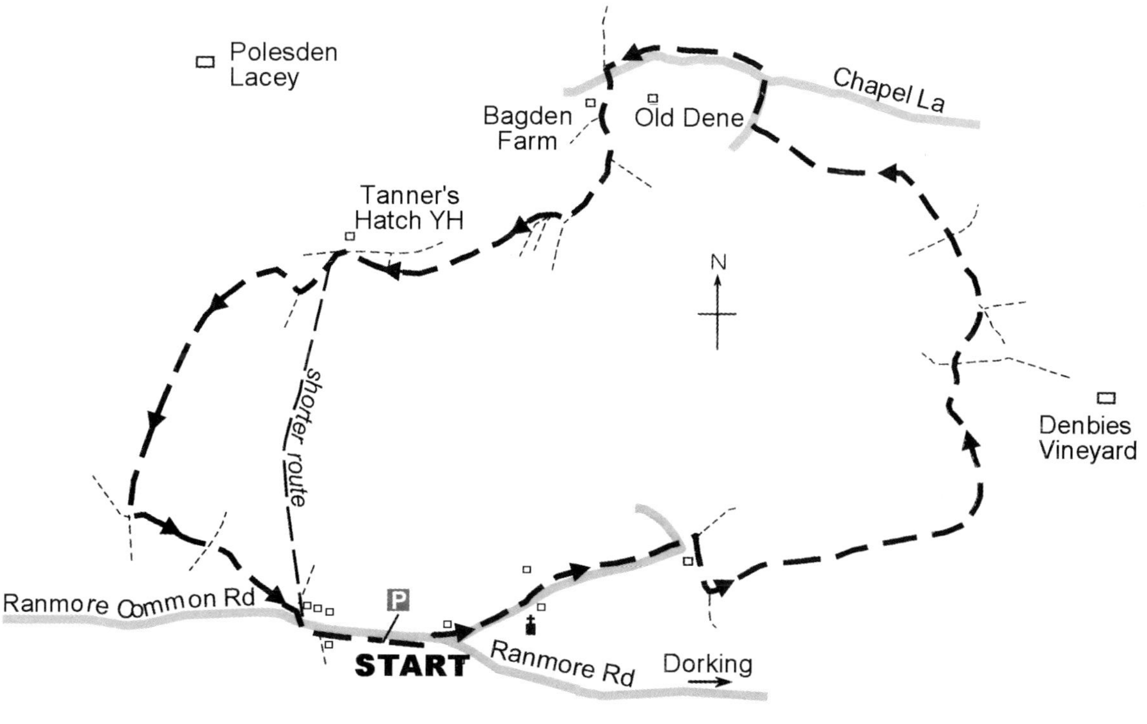

40. WESTCOTT TO WOTTON

Easy, 3 miles.

Combine with Walk 12 for 5 mile walk

Maps SSA P105 D2 OS SSA p135 B5
Park below The Holy Trinity Church, in Logmore Lane at Westcott, but not on Sundays when church is in attendance.

Walk into the church yard via the main gate. Follow the path to the back of the church and up the hill to the top gateway.

Turn immediately right after gate, (before you get to the road side,) along a little track that leads between shrubs then out on to Westcott Heath. Walk on along the green keeping the road and houses left. When the road ends, go straight on, to the footpath that leads downhill through light woodland. This sandy path ends at the entrance to Rookery drive at the side of the A25.

Cross the A25 and take the second lane (Hill Lane) right. Do not follow this lane left. Look instead to the right corner for a footpath sign which leads uphill between houses. Don't be put off by two noisy dogs on right.

The footpath will emerge at a farm track. Turn left and walk along this quiet track enjoying views of the North Downs. When you come to a fork, keep left. When you reach Vale farm, look for a footpath just left of the farm house. The path takes you over 2 stiles in quick succession.

You will see the church on the hill right. Stay on the path that runs along the valley bottom, close to the Church. This leads back to the A25. Cross and walk between the pub right and cottage left until you reach a stile which takes you into a field. Keep to the left fence line and turn left at the corner following the fence and path to a stile.

Once over this stile you will find yourself in Sheep House Green Estate. Keep bearing left until the foot path comes out at Sheephouse Lane. Turn right into the lane and walk about 10 paces looking for a small gap leading to the footpath on the other side of the lane.. This brings you to a fence line after a few paces.

Turn right, keeping the farm and fence left and walk to the end of the field. Here, turn left onto another path that once again runs beside the boundary line. When you come to a junction, go straight across the path that runs left and right and follow the diagonal path (steepish) that heads down hill.

Stay on this path that eventually will lead you to Rookery Hill Farm, a beauty spot at any time of year. After passing between the 2 picturesque cottages, follow their driveway back to the A25. From here retrace your steps up to Westcott Heath and back to the church.

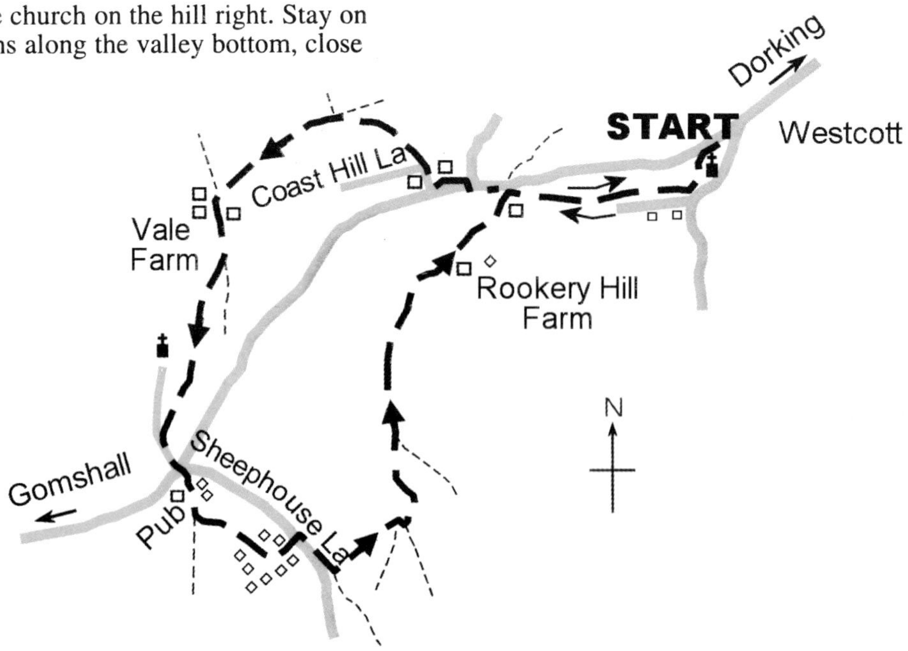